How Tall is This Ghost, John?

How Tall is This Ghost, John?

David Mallick

To my co-author

Acknowledgements
We are grateful to the following for permission to reproduce copyright material:
Edward Arnold for short extracts from John Russell Brown's *Shakespeare's Plays in Performance*; Random House Inc. for a short extract from Richard Sterne's *John Gielgud Directs Richard Burton in Hamlet*; Penguin Books Ltd for a short extract from G. Wilson Knight's *Principles of Shakespearean Production*; Cambridge University Press for short extracts from John Ripley's *Julius Caesar on Stage in England and America 1599–1973* and John Styan's *Shakespeare's Stagecraft*; MacMillan Pty Ltd for short extracts from John Russell Brown's *Discovering Shakespeare*; University of California Press for several short extracts from M. Rosenberg's *The Masks of King Lear* and *The Masks of Macbeth*.

Photography by Doug Nicholas

Published by the Australian Association for the Teaching of English
First published 1984
Copyright © 1984 Australian Association for the Teaching of English
Designed by Publishing Design Studio Pty Ltd, Adelaide
Set in Australia by B&D Modgraphic Pty Ltd
Printed by Hyde Park Press Pty Ltd, Adelaide

National Library of Australia
Cataloguing-in-Publication data
Mallick, David, 1934–.
  How tall is this ghost, John?

  For secondary school students.
  ISBN 0 909955 50 6.

  1. Shakespeare, William, 1564–1616 — Dramatic production — Juvenile literature. I. Title.
792.9

Contents

To the Teachers

The present text is based on the following assumptions:
• Talking is central to English literature lessons. Our earliest critical ideas are best tested in group and class discussion.
• Shakespeare can be managed with pleasure and insight by the average high school student.
• Shakespeare is meant to be performed; practical performance work is the best way to encourage close scrutiny of the text.
• Many English teachers are unsure of how to approach the text as performance, preferring to leave such work to the drama specialist.

In working with my student teachers I spend some time in practical work on scripts. In seminars I lead the initial reading and performance of a selected script. Interpretation arises out of performance: my intention is to convince the teachers that the answer to studying drama lies in making the classroom a workshop where we try to understand meaning through action.

While this approach is usually well received by the teachers, I have observed that often they fail to continue to experiment with it, settling for the sedentary reading and critical analysis which they often remember with dismay from their own school days.

This has led me to believe that what was needed was an account of a sequence of practical drama lessons that would provide teachers and students with a gentle but detailed introduction to reading and performance. Though the examples in this text are confined to scenes from Shakespeare, the ideas and strategies described can be applied to any scripts, including scripts written by class members.

The clue for the work came from a statement by drama critic, H. Granville-Barker. He argued that a play of any quality is "like an iceberg floating one-ninth above the water and eight-ninths submerged; the words on the page represent the one-ninth".

What makes up the other eight-ninths? In Section One I have named some of the more obvious elements: pace, tone, silence, emphasis, stage business, movement, entrances, exits. I have included extracts from the plays for illustration and practice. For each element of the sub-text I have given an example of how I think it could best be performed and read. I must emphasise that the reading is given for comment, discussion, criticism and to provoke further thought. One of the most worthwhile lessons we can convey to a class is that while there is no "right" reading, there are probably inferior ones.

Section Two groups scenes under the thematic headings of: crowds, moments of tension, ghosts, and comic scenes. On the left hand page, instead of the usual scholarly annotations and word meanings, I have included ideas and questions related to all the elements mentioned in Section One, to encourage discussion. Section Three brings together the scenes in *Macbeth* in which Lady Macbeth appears, as a study of the interpretation of a particular character for performance. Again the notes are intended to help in discussion.

For some years we have been emphasising the importance of talk in learning; we have struggled to develop an alternative vision of teaching, substituting the round table for the "disappearing dais". In literature lessons we have become aware of the importance of those first, tentative, partial, and selective responses, arguing that such exploratory talking must be the first step towards less subjective, more refined judgement. Discussion will arise as a result of response to reading or performance. The comments and questions might be simple ones like: "Do you think this line should go like this?"; "I rather like that silence there"; "What if we try it like this?", and so on.

Before a reader responds with, "This is pretty elementary stuff", I want to quote from a book called *John Gielgud Directs Richard Burton in Hamlet*. A member of the cast tape recorded discussions at the rehearsals. The book is written around the transcripts. Here are Gielgud and Burton on the Ghost:

BURTON: I'm not sure what to do when I see the Ghost at this point.

GIELGUD: I'm not either. Let's wait. Something will come when we play it.

BURTON: *How tall is this Ghost, John?*

GIELGUD: My height ... I think you've got to be more hushed and awed when you talk to the Ghost. Save your outbursts for the soliloquy after the next scene when the Ghost is gone.

BURTON: Is the line "I say away" spoken to the Ghost?

GIELGUD: No, it's to them ... Now let's play this Ghost tape. I've left spaces for your lines. Let's see how it works.

Here are the giants of the theatre feeling their way into meaning and performance. Similar intelligent discussion can go on in any classroom.

Section One
Elements of the Sub-text

In this section various elements of the sub-text are identified. Each element is accompanied by two or more passages from a Shakespearean play. With the first passage there is a more detailed examination of the element of the sub-text with reference to the extract. Other passages are quoted to encourage further discussion and to lead into performance.

TONE

A line's full meaning is much more than its sense: that is what it is saying on the page. A considerable amount of meaning will come through the way the line is read, through the tone of the voice. The voice can show a variety and flexibility which can communicate feeling, underline a situation, reveal the mood of a character: in short, working on the sound and rhythm of the line can lead the reader towards the fullest sense which the writer intended.

Take a simple sentence: *I told you not to come.*

It can be said as a menacing warning—it would probably be best said slowly with heavy emphasis on "not" and "come" with the voice trailing off at the end of the sentence.

It can be said laughingly—the line would be spoken quickly with laughter breaking in over the last word.

It can be said with resignation—the sentence would be long and labouring, breaking off into an almost inaudible sigh.

Exercises

1. Say each of the following lines harshly, tenderly and with resignation.
   • This is it.
   • Don't cry.
2. In what situations can the following pieces of dialogue be said? How does the tone change with the situation?
   A: How long?
   B: Two minutes.
   A: He's been gone one hour.
   B: Yes.
   A: So?

King Lear 1 (Act I Scene I)

King Lear is an ageing autocratic monarch. He has three daughters: Goneril, Regan and Cordelia. He decides, partly for selfish reasons, and partly because he is getting old, to divide his kingdom among his daughters. At the beginning of the play he asks his daughters to tell him how much they love him. Goneril and Regan finish their flattering speeches, and it is Cordelia's turn. Just before this, in an aside, Cordelia murmurs: "What shall Cordelia do? Love and be silent".

LEAR: Now, our joy,
    Although our last and least—to whose young love
    The vines of France and milk of Burgundy
    Strive to be interess'd. What can you say to draw
    A third more opulent than your sisters'? Speak.
CORDELIA: Nothing, my lord.
LEAR: Nothing?
CORDELIA: Nothing.
LEAR: Nothing will come of nothing. Speak again.

CORDELIA: Unhappy that I am, I cannot heave
　　　My heart into my mouth. I love your majesty
　　　According to my bond, no more nor less.
LEAR: How, how, Cordelia? Mend your speech a little
　　　Lest you may mar your fortunes.
CORDELIA: 　　　　　　　　　　　Good my lord,
　　　You have begot me, bred me, lov'd me.
　　　I return those duties back as are right fit—
　　　Obey you, love you, and most honour you.
　　　Why have my sisters husbands, if they say
　　　They love you all? Happily when I shall wed,
　　　That lord whose hand must take my plight shall carry
　　　Half my love with him, half my care and duty:
　　　Sure I shall never marry like my sisters,
　　　To love my father all.
LEAR: But goes thy heart with this?
CORDELIA: 　　　　　　　　　　Ay, my good lord.
LEAR: So young and so untender?
CORDELIA: So young, my lord, and true.

Tonally there are two very important sentences here: "Speak", and "Nothing, my lord".

What should be the tone of "Speak"? There are at least three possibilities:

- Without pausing between "sisters" and "Speak", he says it in a matter-of-fact way.
- There is a pause between the two words and he says "Speak" in a surprised way.
- There is a long pause between the two words and he breathes out a hissed warning.

The third seems the most successful. It could be a hiss between clenched teeth or a low, growling threat. What is important is that there should be a threatening tone. Why? Lear has grown accustomed to the flattery of the other sisters but here, in the silence, there is a sudden realisation of danger, the danger of his daughter opposing him.

Look at Cordelia's response, "Nothing, my lord". Remembering her first aside "What shall Cordelia do. . .", it seems that her first reply should be no answer at all. A long silence seems most suitable. The seconds pass and she says nothing. Then Lear forces her with his threatening command. What tone should her reply take? She could answer with fire, or nervously, or curtly. Apart from the fact that the rest of the play emphasises her gentle strength, a whispered, deeply felt response contrasts well with the rising anger in Lear's speech.

Do you agree with the above reading?

Are there other lines where you think the tone of the voice could be very significant?

Does the tone of Cordelia's lines change? What does the tone show of her mental state?

LEAR: Out of my sight!

King Lear 2 (Act I, Scene I)
Cordelia refuses to flatter her father and Lear goes into a furious rage. He refuses to give any of his kingdom to her, dividing it up between the other two sisters. Lear's friend, Kent, sees the injustice of the act, knowing that Cordelia has responded truthfully. Lear in his rage will not be appeased.

KENT: Royal Lear,
 Whom I have ever honour'd as my king,
 Lov'd as my father, as my master follow'd,
 As my great patron thought on in my prayers—

LEAR: The bow is bent and drawn: make from the shaft.
KENT: Let it fall rather, though the fork invade
    The region of my heart. Be Kent unmannerly
    When Lear is mad. What wouldst thou do, old man?
    Think'st thou that duty shall have dread to speak
    When power to flattery bows? To plainness honour's bound   10
    When majesty falls to folly. Reserve thy state,
    And, in thy best consideration, check
    This hideous rashness. Answer my life my judgement,
    Thy youngest daughter does not love thee least,
    Nor are those empty-hearted whose low sounds
    Reverb no hollowness.
LEAR: Kent, on thy life, no more.
KENT: My life I never held but as a pawn
    To wage against thine enemies—nor fear to lose it,
    Thy safety being motive.   20
LEAR: Out of my sight!
KENT: See better, Lear, and let me still remain
    The true blank of thine eye.
LEAR: Now, by Apollo—
KENT: Now, by Apollo, King,
    Thou swear'st thy gods in vain.
LEAR: *[making for his sword]*   O vassal! miscreant!
ALBANY AND CORNWALL: Dear sir, forbear!
KENT: Kill thy physician, and thy fee bestow
    Upon the foul disease? Revoke thy gift,   30
    Or whilst I can vent clamour from my throat
    I'll tell thee thou dost evil.

Do you agree with the following description of the way the scene should be read?

    ... a normal rhythm would raise Lear to a pitch higher than his excitement over Cordelia, to give him the outlet for physical violence with his sword. The pitch of fury of even the most outraged Lear needs some tempering at the outset. Gielgud's first rebuff, "Kent, on thy life, no more" was dead quiet. Lear merely turned and stared at him.

                      M. Rosenberg, *The Masks of King Lear*

Look at Line 4. Is the dash after Kent's line "As my great patron..." important? What about the dash after Lear's line "Now, by Apollo"?

What lines show Lear's mounting rage? Can changes in tone show the stages of his increasing rage?

Read Lines 6–16. Mark in where there could be any change of tone in Kent's speech.

What can be made of the word "King" in Line 25?

TIMING—PACING

In simple terms, timing and pacing concern the rate at which the lines are read. But it is much more than that: it is a vital and subtle element in reading well. It involves the speed or the slowness of the delivery but also concerns the length and the number of pauses. Even more, it reveals what is happening between the people in a situation at any particular moment. A change of pace can affect the mood and force of a scene and can affect how we see characters.

Exercises

1. Take the following piece of dialogue:
    A: My God he's coming.
    B: I can see him.
    If the speakers wish to express joy at someone coming the lines would probably be said very quickly. How would the pace vary if the situation demanded an expression of fear or grief or indifference?
      Take other pairs of sentences and practise reading them at a different pace.
2. Write short speeches for the following situations:
    • A political speech: you are trying to whip the crowd into a frenzy.
    • A speech at a funeral.
    Practise reading the speeches in a way which is designed to make the greatest appeal to the audience.
3. Make up a speech in nonsense words. Deliver the speech to the class concentrating on timing and pacing. If the tempo has been carefully worked on the class should be able to guess the situation.

Hamlet 1 (Act V, Scene I)
The King of Denmark is dead; his ghost appears to Hamlet, his son, and speaks. Hamlet learns that Claudius has murdered the King in order to succeed him on the throne. He has married Hamlet's mother, Gertrude, the King's widow. Hamlet is stricken by the news; some think he is mad. Ophelia is disturbed by his strange behaviour, and his rejection of her love. She commits suicide.

  The following incident occurs at the burial of Ophelia. Laertes, her brother, the King, the Queen and courtiers are at the graveside. Hamlet appears and begins to fight with Laertes.

HAMLET: This is I,
    Hamlet the Dane.
                          [Leaps in after Laertes]
LAERTES: The devil take thy soul!
                          [Grapples with him]
HAMLET: Thou pray'st not well.
    I prithee take thy fingers from my throat,

6

For, though I am not splenitive and rash,
Yet have I in me something dangerous,
Which let thy wisdom fear. Hold off thy hand.

KING: Pluck them asunder.

QUEEN: Hamlet, Hamlet!

ALL: Gentlemen!

HORATIO: Good my lord, be quiet.

[Attendants part them, and they come out of the grave]

HAMLET: Why, I will fight with him upon this theme
Until my eyelids will no longer wag.

QUEEN: O my son, what theme?

HAMLET: I loved Ophelia.

The lines must be read in a way that conveys the horror and confusion of the scene. Two men—a lover and a brother—are fighting over a dead body. The violence of the action must be heard in the shouting and confusion of the lines. The short lines signal a rising pitch and a quickening pace.

But what happens to the pace of the scene in the last two lines? There are two possible interpretations worth working on and the answer depends on what is going through Hamlet's mind at the moment.

• When he says "I loved Ophelia", he may look at his mother as if he cannot believe his ears that she can be so dull-witted not to understand. In that case the pace would continue and he would bark the line at his mother.

• On the other hand, a more moving reading, (and it shows how dramatic a change of pace can be), is that after the sudden rush of feeling and the violent shouting from those at the grave, he suddenly hears his mother's question. What happens between the word "theme" and the word "I"? He suddenly realises how much he loves Ophelia, pauses, and with quiet simplicity, as much to himself as to his mother, he murmurs, "I loved Ophelia."

The pause changes the whole pace of the scene and there is a corresponding change of mood and tone; the pause and the quiet line emphasise Hamlet's deep grief.

Hamlet 2 (Act I, Scene II)

This is a scene from earlier in the play. The ghost of the King has first appeared to Horatio, a friend of Hamlet, and to Bernardo and Marcellus, two officers. The three men go to tell Hamlet of the strange appearance of the ghost of his father.

HAMLET: 'Tis very strange.

HORATIO: As I do live, my honoured lord, 'tis true,
And we did think it writ down in our duty
To let you know of it.

HAMLET: Indeed, indeed, sirs, but this troubles me.
Hold you the watch tonight?

ALL: We do, my lord.

HAMLET: Armed, say you?

ALL: Armed, my lord.

HAMLET: From top to toe?   10

ALL: My lord, from head to foot.

HAMLET: Then saw you not his face?

HORATIO: O, yes, my lord. He wore his beaver up.

HAMLET: What, looked he frowningly?

HORATIO: A countenance more in sorrow than in anger.

HAMLET: Pale or red?

HORATIO: Nay, very pale.

HAMLET: And fixed his eyes upon you?

HORATIO: Most constantly.

HAMLET: I would I had been there.   20

HORATIO: It would have much amazed you.

HAMLET: Very like, very like. Stayed it long?

HORATIO: While one with moderate haste might tell a hundred.

BOTH: Longer, longer.

HORATIO: Not when I saw't.

HAMLET: His beard was grizzled, no?

HORATIO: It was as I have seen it in his life,
    A sable silvered.

HAMLET: I will watch tonight.
    Perchance 'twill walk again.   30

HORATIO: I warr'nt it will.

HAMLET: If it assume my noble father's person,
    I'll speak to it though hell itself should gape
    And bid me hold my peace.

Take a section of the scene and speak it as quickly as possible. Then speak it as slowly as possible. Divide the section according to the following and practise a reading:
• Some lines increase in pace to show excitement.
• Some lines require a pause and a quiet voice.
• Some lines require firmness and decision.
Would you agree with the following drama critic's views on the scene?

If the audience is to catch the excitement when Hamlet faces the implications of seeing his father's ghost, the preparatory cross-questioning of his friends must increase its pace in a crescendo:

"HAMLET: Armed, say you?

ALL: Armed, my lord.

HAMLET: From top to toe?

ALL: My lord, from head to foot.

HAMLET: Then saw you not his face?

HORATIO: O, yes, my lord. He wore his beaver up."

At this, the Prince's sudden challenge to Horatio— "Then saw you not his face"—is logically answered, and it suggests a momentary pause before he pursues a new line of thinking and the pace accelerates again:

"HAMLET: What, looked he frowningly?
HORATIO: A countenance more in sorrow than in anger.
HAMLET: Pale or red?
HORATIO: Nay, very pale."

Only the reflective "I would I had been there" breaks the run before the clinching decision, "I will watch tonight", and after this Hamlet halts the sequence by the firm lines of verse with which he orders the men to meet him.

J. L. Styan, *Shakespeare's Stagecraft*

Hamlet 3 (Act V, Scene II)
This extract comes from the last scene of the play. Claudius plans to kill Hamlet because he fears he knows the truth. He plots the murder with Laertes. They arrange a sporting sword fight between Hamlet and Laertes in which Laertes will put a deadly poison on the tip of his sword. To make sure of Hamlet's death Claudius will put poison in Hamlet's cup of wine. During the duel the Queen drinks from the poisoned cup and Hamlet and Laertes, in the confusion, exchange swords. At the moment of death Laertes tells Hamlet that the sword is poisoned and that Claudius is responsible.

KING: Give me the cups,
     And let the kettle to the trumpet speak,
     The trumpet to the cannoneer without,
     The cannons to the heavens, the heaven to earth,
     "Now the king drinks to Hamlet". Come, begin.

                    [Trumpets the while]

     And you, the judges, bear a wary eye.
HAMLET: Come on, sir.
LAERTES: Come, my lord.

                    [They play]

HAMLET: One.
LAERTES: No.   10
HAMLET: Judgement?
OSRIC: A hit, a very palpable hit.

          [Drum, trumpets, and shot. Flourish; a piece goes off]

LAERTES: Well, again.
KING: Stay, give me drink. Hamlet, this pearl is thine.
     Here's to thy health. Give him the cup.
HAMLET: I'll play this bout first; set it by awhile.
     Come. *[They play]* Another hit. What say you?
LAERTES: A touch, a touch; I do confess't.
KING: Our son shall win.
QUEEN: He's fat, and scant of breath.   20
     Here, Hamlet, take my napkin, rub thy brows.
     The queen carouses to thy fortune, Hamlet.
HAMLET: Good madam!

KING: Gertrude, do not drink.
QUEEN: I will, my lord; I pray you pardon me.

[Drinks]

KING *[aside]*:   It is the poisoned cup; it is too late.
HAMLET: I dare not drink yet, madam—by and by.
QUEEN: Come, let me wipe thy face.
LAERTES: My lord, I'll hit him now.
KING: I do not think't.   30
LAERTES *[aside]*:   And yet it is almost against my conscience.
HAMLET: Come for the third, Laertes. You but dally.
   I pray you pass with your best violence;
   I am afeard you make a wanton of me.
LAERTES: Say you so? Come on.

[They play]

OSRIC: Nothing neither way.
LAERTES: Have at you now!

*[In scuffling they change rapiers, and both are
wounded with the poisoned weapon]*

KING: Part them. They are incensed.
HAMLET: Nay, come—again!

[The Queen falls]

OSRIC: Look to the queen there, ho!   40
HORATIO: They bleed on both sides. How is it, my lord?
OSRIC: How is't, Laertes?
LAERTES: Why, as a woodcock to mine own springe, Osric.
   I am justly killed with mine own treachery.
HAMLET: How does the queen?
KING: She sounds to see them bleed.
QUEEN: No, no, the drink, the drink! O my dear Hamlet!
   The drink, the drink! I am poisoned.

[Dies]

HAMLET: O villainy! Ho! let the door be locked.
   Treachery! Seek it out.   50

[Laertes falls]

LAERTES: It is here, Hamlet. Hamlet, thou art slain;
   No med'cine in the world can do thee good.
   In thee there is not half an hour's life.
   The treacherous instrument is in thy hand,
   Unbated and envenomed. The foul practice
   Hath turned itself on me. Lo, here I lie,
   Never to rise again. Thy mother's poisoned.
   I can no more. The king, the king's to blame.
HAMLET: The point envenomed too?
   Then venom, to thy work.   60

[Hurts the King]

10

ALL: Treason! treason!

KING: O, yet defend me, friends. I am but hurt.

HAMLET: Here, thou incestuous, murd'rous, damnèd Dane,
Drink off this potion. Is thy union here?
Follow my mother.

[King dies]

LAERTES: He is justly served.
It is a poison tempered by himself.
Exchange forgiveness with me, noble Hamlet.
Mine and my father's death come not upon thee,
Nor thine on me!

[Dies]

Success in reading the scene will depend upon changes in pace and timing. But to get these right you should be aware of the following:

- The grouping of the characters.
- The sword fight with its silences and sudden excitement.
- The confusion on the deaths.

Here is the way a famous producer, John Gielgud, worked on the scene:

When a thorough rehearsal of the final court scene began, everything went wrong. Gielgud started by placing the Queen on one side of the stage and the King on the platform above her. When this was arranged, the King gave the line "Give me the cups", but the wine cups were on the opposite side of the stage. "Oh, what a terrible director I am!" Gielgud said in desperation. He started from the beginning with a complete restaging, only to have similar problems arise.

Drake asked that he be placed closer to the Queen after she takes the cup.

Gielgud asked Drake what he thought of having the King at the end of the scene accept his imminent death openly, realising that there was no escaping it, but Drake pointed out that this was counter to his line "O, yet defend me, friends".

Returning to the duel between Laertes and Hamlet, Burton suggested that in the exchange of rapiers the traditional staging of having Hamlet violently beat the poisoned rapier out of Laertes' hand be eliminated. He preferred that Hamlet very quietly and with no struggle should simply walk up to Laertes and take the weapon from him deliberately.

R. Sterne, *John Gielgud Directs Richard Burton in Hamlet*

PAUSE—SILENCE

The dramatic life of any scene lies in its moments of silence as well as in its words and actions. Of course it is not silence for its own sake, but a silence that grows out of the moment in the scene and provides the tension in the situation.

How long should a pause be? Part of the answer to that lies in the degree of dramatic value of the line or action which goes immediately before it. As a general rule the more powerful or more stunning the preceding line or action the longer the pause.

What is achieved by the silence?

- It gives an audience time to react to a situation, action or line.
- It emphasises the line or action that has just gone before.
- It creates a feeling of suspense that prepares us for the next line.

Exercises

1. A parent has caught a child apparently stealing.

   PARENT: Have you been touching that money box?
   Silence.
   PARENT: I said have you been touching that money box?
   Silence.
   CHILD: Yes.

   Develop the conversation. Relevant pauses and moments of silence add strength to the case against or in favour of the child.

2. A soldier has captured an enemy. He guards him while waiting for his company to arrive. They are together for five minutes. It is likely that they will not immediately start to talk. What forces them to begin? What kinds of things will they talk about? What can the pauses and silences suggest about the men, their relationship, the situation?

Macbeth 1 (Act IV Scene III)

Macbeth, aided by his wife, Lady Macbeth, has murdered Duncan, King of Scotland. He becomes King. In order to keep his power he murders any who oppose him. Finally he resorts to killing women and children. One of his opponents is Macduff who has fled from Scotland, leaving his family behind, thinking they would be safe. Macbeth has Macduff's wife and children murdered. Two friends of Macduff, Ross and Malcolm, visit him to break the terrible news.

MACDUFF: If it be mine,
    Keep it not from me, quickly let me have it.
ROSS: Let not your ears despise my tongue for ever,
    Which shall possess them with the heaviest sound
    That ever yet they heard.
MACDUFF: Humh! I guess at it.
ROSS: Your castle is surprised; your wife and babes
    Savagely slaughtered. To relate the manner,

> Were on the quarry of these murdered deer
> To add the death of you.   10
> MALCOLM: Merciful heaven!
> What man, ne'er pull your hat upon your brows,
> Give sorrow words; the grief that does not speak
> Whispers the o'er-fraught heart, and bids it break.
> MACDUFF: My children too?
> ROSS: Wife, children, servants, all
> That could be found.
> MACDUFF: And I must be from thence!
> My wife killed too?
> ROSS: I have said.   20
> MALCOLM: Be comforted.
> Let's make us medicines of our great revenge,
> To cure this deadly grief.
> MACDUFF: He has no children. All my pretty ones?
> Did you say all? O hell-kite! All?
> What, all my pretty chickens and their dam
> At one fell swoop?

There are several places here where a pause may be justified but there is one occasion when it is not only justified but essential. Just after Ross breaks the news Malcolm says "Give sorrow words". Macduff is silent. The news has shattered him.

It is worthwhile working on where to place the silence to give it the greatest impact. If it is put after "To add the death of you" there is a suggestion that Malcolm finds the silence too pitiful and he turns on Macduff urging him to pull himself together.

On the other hand, it could come after "Merciful heaven!". This would suggest that Malcolm himself is overcome at the horror of the news and the effect it has on Macduff. This would probably change the tone of the line "Merciful heaven!". He would whisper it softly in his own anguish.

In the rest of the scene we must sense a growing movement in Macduff's lines from the pathos of the murmured "My children too?" to the despair of the unbelieving question "My wife killed too?" to the powerful determination beginning in "O hell-kite!". These lines would be punctuated by short but significant pauses as each moment leaves Macduff with a new heart-breaking realisation.

Physical action can help shape the pausing and the length of the pauses. Possibilities are:
• As Macduff hears the news he draws away in solitary grief.
• On the line "My wife killed too?" he returns to the centre and picks up his sword. He is prepared for revenge.

Macbeth 2 (Act V, Scene II)
Things are closing in on Macbeth. The witches have prophesised that Macbeth cannot be killed till a forest at Birnam wood moves and also that

he cannot be killed by any man born of a woman. But he keeps receiving news that greater forces are being built up to invade Scotland and depose him from the throne. Here we have Macbeth thinking on the situation. A servant brings more news about the opposing armies.

MACBETH: Bring me no more reports, let them fly all.
Till Birnam wood remove to Dunsinane,
I cannot taint with fear. What's the boy Malcolm?
Was he not born of woman? The spirits that know
All mortal consequences have pronounced me thus:
"Fear not Macbeth, no man that's born of woman
Shall e'er have power upon thee". Then fly false thanes,
And mingle with the English epicures.
The mind I sway by, and the heart I bear,
Shall never sag with doubt, nor shake with fear.   10

[Enter a Servant]

The devil damn thee black, thou cream-faced loon.
Where gott'st thou that goose look?
SERVANT: There is ten thousand—
MACBETH: Geese, villain?
SERVANT: Soldiers sir.
MACBETH: Go prick thy face, and over-red thy fear,
Thou lily-livered boy. What soldiers, patch?
Death of thy soul, those linen cheeks of thine
Are counsellors to fear. What soldiers, whey-face?
SERVANT: The English force, so please you.   20
MACBETH: Take thy face hence.

[Exit Servant]

                          Seyton!—I am sick at heart,
When I behold—Seyton, I say!—This push
Will cheer me ever, or disseat me now.
I have lived long enough. My way of life
Is fallen into the sear, the yellow leaf;
And that which should accompany old age,
As honour, love, obedience, troops of friends,
I must not look to have; but in their stead
Curses, not loud but deep, mouth-honour, breath,   30
Which the poor heart would fain deny, and dare not.
Seyton!

There are contrasting emotions here and they require different qualities of tone, rate of speaking and length of pause. Mark in:
• Where there is a change of mood.
• Where a pause would emphasise or introduce that change of mood.

Here is one drama critic on part of the speech where Macbeth speaks to himself:

But the breaks in speech direction are well enough explained as reflections of the zigzag of Macbeth's mind:
"Seyton",
the command is shouted; but the old raptness is coming on—
"I am sick at heart,
When I behold":
Pause, the thought remains unfaced, as the brain fires across; back to the summons:
"Seyton, I say!"

M. Rosenberg, The Masks of Macbeth

Macbeth 3 (Act V Scene V)

Macbeth is faced with a worsening situation. He is continually hearing news that the war is going badly, and finally, as he urges on his troops, he has news of his wife's death.

MACBETH: Hang out our banners on the outward walls.
　　　The cry is still "They come". Our castle's strength
　　　Will laugh a siege to scorn. Here let them lie
　　　Till famine and the ague eat them up.
　　　Were they not forced with those that should be ours,
　　　We might have met them dareful, beard to beard,
　　　And beat them backward home.

[A cry of women within]

　　　　　　　　　What is that noise?
SEYTON: It is the cry of women, my good lord.

[Exit]

MACBETH: I have almost forgot the taste of fears.　　　　　　　10
　　　The time has been, my senses would have cooled
　　　To hear a night-shriek, and my fell of hair
　　　Would at a dismal treatise rouse and stir
　　　As life were in't. I have supped full with horrors;
　　　Direness, familiar to my slaughterous thoughts
　　　Cannot once start me.

[Enter Seyton]

　　　　　　　Wherefore was that cry?
SEYTON: The Queen, my lord, is dead.
MACBETH: She should have died hereafter;
　　　There would have been a time for such a word.　　　　　20
　　　Tomorrow, and tomorrow, and tomorrow,
　　　Creeps in this petty pace from day to day,
　　　To the last syllable of recorded time;
　　　And all our yesterdays have lighted fools
　　　The way to dusty death. Out, out, brief candle!
　　　Life's but a walking shadow, a poor player,
　　　That struts and frets his hour upon the stage,

And then is heard no more. It is a tale
Told by an idiot, full of sound and fury,   30
Signifying nothing.

One drama critic wrote: "Macbeth's reflections upon his Queen's death are the final stillness of despair".

Mark in where there should be pauses and practise reading to show "the stillness of despair".

Another drama critic wrote:

Scofield [the actor] seemed to look into a hereafter when Lady Macbeth might still be alive to him; his stern voice softened with compassion—for fools, for himself—and a touch of longing.

M. Rosenberg, *The Masks of Macbeth*

Practise reading the speeches to bring out the "compassion… and a touch of longing".

EMPHASIS AND PROGRESSION

A good reading requires careful handling of sentences so that words are constantly moving towards a focal point. We must feel that the lines are going somewhere and are thus following the progression of thought and feeling that keeps an audience listening.

Selecting the words to be emphasised is an important factor in interpreting the lines. This selection is determined by the meaning of the words and what is happening in the scene. But what is also important is the way a scene builds up in power.

As an emotional scene runs towards its climax it increases in speed and volume and rises in pitch. But it is very difficult for the human voice to maintain an increase through an entire scene. There are times when you will indulge in a sort of "breather" in which your energies are recouped and after which you move towards the climax with renewed vigour. These "breathers", when taken in the right place, can be very dramatic.

Exercises

1. There is an argument in the street. It starts slowly and builds up to a climax. How does it finish? Perhaps it could finish in a fight; or perhaps the parties settle their differences; or it might peter out.
2. Write a political speech. Practise reading the speech to the class, building a progression through increase in pitch, volume, rate; you are aiming to have your audience in sympathy with you whatever they think of the information in the speech.
3. Write a short speech that will be delivered furiously or sarcastically or threateningly or haughtily or nonchalantly.
4. Write short speeches which will express the tone of command of a sergeant major, a headmaster, or a master to his servant.

Othello 1 (Act III, Scene IV)
Othello, a black Moor and a brave soldier, marries Desdemona, a beautiful and gracious woman. Othello's closest friend is Cassio, who has been a go-between in his courting of Desdemona. Othello has promoted Cassio in the army and this promotion has aroused the hatred of Iago. Iago hates both Cassio and Othello. He plans to make Othello jealous of Cassio, and lays many plots to entrap Desdemona. One of his ploys is eventually successful. Iago tells Othello that he has seen Cassio with a handkerchief that Othello has once given Desdemona. The truth is that Iago's wife has stolen the handkerchief. Othello flies into a rage. In the following scene Othello is asking for the handkerchief, and Desdemona, who knows nothing about the plot, is confused by his anger.

OTHELLO: Is't lost? Is't gone? Speak: is't out o'th'way?
DESDEMONA: Heaven bless us!
OTHELLO: Say you?
DESDEMONA: It is not lost.
But what an if it were?

OTHELLO: How!

DESDEMONA: I say it is not lost.

OTHELLO: Fetch't: let me see't.

DESDEMONA: Why, so I can, sir; but I will not now.
  This is a trick to put me from my suit.   10
  Pray you let Cassio be received again.

OTHELLO: Fetch me the handkerchief: my mind misgives.

DESDEMONA: Come, come:
  You'll never meet a more sufficient man.

OTHELLO: The handkerchief!

DESDEMONA: I pray, talk me of Cassio.

OTHELLO: The handkerchief!

DESDEMONA: A man that all his time
  Hath founded his good fortunes on your love;
  Shared dangers with you—   20

OTHELLO: The handkerchief!

DESDEMONA: I'faith you are to blame.

OTHELLO: Away!

[Exit]

The terror of the scene must be achieved by the fury of the words that Othello flings at Desdemona. The more interesting words are the repetitions of "handkerchief" and the final "Away!". The question to experiment with is whether the scene should progress upwards or downwards; whether the first line should be murmured and threatening, rising to a crescendo of fierce bitterness, or whether it should start off with a vengeance and then die down.

It is probable the first is the more suitable, not only because that is the way an accusation should go but also because a thundering last "handkerchief" gives us room to play with the word "Away". "Away" is not just an expression of exasperation. The repetition of "handkerchief" reveals that Othello's anger has mounted to such a pitch that he can go no further. The last line is breathed out with a vicious hatred and he stumbles away.

The following notes on this scene were written by the Russian director, Stanislavsky, for his production of *Othello*:

OTHELLO: *The handkerchief!*

Othello interrupts her, not allowing her to finish.

The actor will have to repeat the word "The handkerchief!" three times. There must be an intensification, and it must be done clearly and impressively, but remember, there is much intensification of this kind still ahead. In cases like this when one does not wish to strangle the temperament which is bound to carry you away, and yet keep it from exhausting itself, one will have to resort to coverings. One of them would be intense inner suffering (which is the sordine), and not just wrath acted on pure temperament and high voltage.

DESDEMONA: *I pray, talk me of Cassio.*

Now Desdemona cannot stop any more, driven on by the nervous state of mind, the whole scene and confusion. Now her embarrassment makes

18

her go on talking, just as it reduced her to silence before. Her eyes are on Othello like those of a frightened child who cannot stop for fear of bursting into tears.

OTHELLO: *The handkerchief!*

What can be placed beneath these exclamations "The handkerchief!" to make them more effective? Another warning—Othello is implying as it were: "I warn you, no tricks will help you!" or: "Bear in mind, truth is the only thing that can save you!" If even more covering is needed, one could entreat Desdemona to tell the truth instead of warning her, using the same grade of temperament.

If, on the other hand, intensification is needed (not of the kind, however, that will be required in the following act) one should make a definite request, saying: "The handkerchief!"—and no more excuses.

Or all this screening of the temperament could be done in the order of intensification, i.e. the first exclamation "The handkerchief!" as an entreaty, the second—warning, the third—a definite request.

DESDEMONA: *A man that all his time.*

The longer Desdemona pleads her case for Cassio, the more she becomes embarrassed, helpless and at a loss.

Hath founded his good fortunes on your love;
Shared dangers with you—

OTHELLO: *The handkerchief!*

After the third and most powerful exclamation "The handkerchief!" is a pause. Both are surprised and embarrassed at the fact that they have reached such a tone so soon.

Confused pause. They look at each other in astonishment and cannot adapt themselves to this new relationship.

Othello tries to calm down and repair what has been done.

DESDEMONA: *I' faith, you are to blame.*

Desdemona makes a slight attempt of reconciliation. In addition to the words she speaks and the intonation she used she tries to go up to him and makes not even a step, only a movement, in his direction, but...

OTHELLO: *Away!*

[Exit]

Othello 2 (Act V, Scene II)
Othello's suspicions increase and his rage grows. He finally murders Desdemona.

OTHELLO: He hath confessed.
DESDEMONA: What, my lord?
OTHELLO: That he hath used thee.
DESDEMONA: How? Unlawfully?
OTHELLO: Ay.
DESDEMONA: He will not say so.
OTHELLO: No, his mouth is stopped:
   Honest Iago hath ta'en order for't.

DESDEMONA: O, my fear interprets! What, is he dead?
OTHELLO: Had all his hairs been lives, my great revenge   10
　　　Had stomach for them all.
DESDEMONA: Alas, he is betrayed, and I undone.
OTHELLO: Out, strumpet! Weep'st thou for him to my face?
DESDEMONA: O banish me, my lord, but kill me not!
OTHELLO: Down, strumpet!
DESDEMONA: Kill me tomorrow: let me live tonight!
OTHELLO: Nay, if you strive—
DESDEMONA: But half an hour!
OTHELLO: 　　　Being done, there is no pause.
DESDEMONA: But while I say one prayer!   20
OTHELLO: 　　　　　It is too late.
DESDEMONA: O Lord, Lord, Lord!

[He smothers her]

Study the producer's notes made by Stanislavsky. Make your own notes on each of the lines in this scene. This exercise can be used with any of the scenes in the book.

DESDEMONA: Kill me tomorrow: let me live tonight!

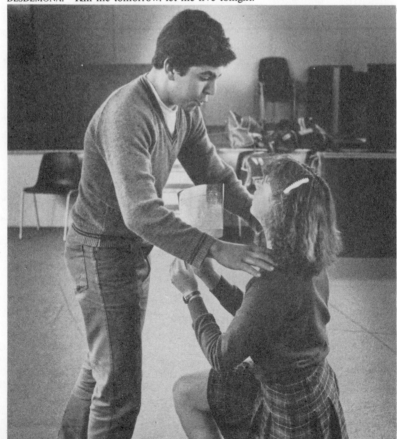

ACTIONS—ESSENTIAL AND INTERPRETATIVE

Drama involves words and action. The words on the page that seem so flatly there are not all there is. Under any printed dialogue are layers of meaning that can never be captured by words alone. Actions (often called stage business) accompanying the words can add considerably to the meaning.

We can distinguish two kinds of actions—essential and interpretative. Essential actions are those which must be included for the words to make sense. Interpretative actions are those which the actor introduces to add colour and depth to the performance. They are appropriate for the lines, the character, and the situation but they are not necessary for it to make sense.

Exercises

1. Read the following piece of dialogue in pairs:

    A: I must be going.
    B: I'll get your hat.
    A: I'll get it.
    B: No please.
      There you are.
    A: Well—goodbye.

    [Exit]

    In this short piece there are two essential actions:
    - B goes to get the hat and returns to give it to A.
    - A must leave at the end.

    But what if the scene concerns two people in a sorrowful parting and we wish to show sadness and reluctance in the farewell? How can we show this sadness in action? As B hands the hat to A, A moves to the door. He stops, looks back and there is a short silence. A returns to B, gently takes her hand and quietly murmurs "Well—goodbye".
    In what way could other situations change the actions?

2. Study the following piece of dialogue. There are five characters.

    A: This wood's damned hard.
    C: It's not as if the bloke's a big fella either.
    B: You've got to use the best.
    E: Anyone'd think you were paying for it.
    A: I hate these rush jobs.
    B: You hate any job, you do.
    D: Never mind, mate—double pay.
    E: You *need* double pay for this sort of work.
    C: What's 'e s'posed to 've done?
    D: What's it matter—it's all trade.

    Decide on the following:
    - Who are they?   • Where are they?
    - What are they doing?   • Why are they doing it?

    Prepare an acted reading of the lines.

King Lear 1 (Act IV, Scene VII)

After being rejected by his daughters Lear goes through a terrible period
of madness. But the madness changes him from an arrogant domineering
father and king to a gentle and humble man. In this scene he is just waking
from a deep sleep after his period of madness. The cruel father is now
with the daughter whom he rejected.

CORDELIA: How does my royal lord? How fares your majesty?

LEAR: You do me wrong to take me out o' th' grave.
    Thou art a soul in bliss, but I am bound
    Upon a wheel of fire, that mine own tears
    Do scald like molten lead.

CORDELIA: Sir, do you know me?

LEAR: You are a spirit, I know. Where did you die?

CORDELIA: Still, still far wide.

DOCTOR: He's scarce awake. Let him alone awhile.

LEAR: Where have I been? Where am I? Fair daylight?   10
    I am mightily abus'd. I should ev'n die with pity
    To see another thus. I know not what to say.
    I will not swear these are my hands. Let's see—
    I feel this pin prick. Would I were assur'd
    Of my condition.

CORDELIA: O look upon me, sir,
    And hold your hand in benediction o'er me.

                    [Lear kneels before her]

    You must not kneel!

LEAR: Pray, do not mock me.
    I am a very foolish fond old man,   20
    Four score and upward, not an hour more nor less,
    And, to deal plainly,
    I fear I am not in my perfect mind.
    Methinks I should know you, and know this man,
    Yet I am doubtful: for I am mainly ignorant
    What place this is, and all the skill I have
    Remembers not these garments; nor I know not
    Where I did lodge last night. Do not laugh at me,
    For, as I am a man, I think this lady
    To be my child Cordelia.   30

CORDELIA: *[weeping]*   And so I am, I am.

LEAR: Be your tears wet? Yes, faith. I pray, weep not.
    If you have poison for me, I will drink it.
    I know you do not love me, for your sisters
    Have, as I do remember, done me wrong:
    You have some cause, they have not.

CORDELIA: No cause, no cause.

LEAR: Am I in France?

KENT: In your own kingdom, sir.

LEAR: Do not abuse me.   40

DOCTOR: Be comforted, good madam. The great rage,
    You see, is kill'd in him, and yet it is danger
    To make him even o'er the time he has lost.
    Desire him to go in. Trouble him no more
    Till further settling.

CORDELIA: Will't please your highness walk?

LEAR: You must bear with me. Pray you now, forget
    and forgive: I am old and foolish.

[Exeunt all but Kent and gentleman]

The text requires actions which show great weariness and grief. The lines give us some clues. Lear must look in sad puzzlement at his hands and in a child-like way he tests his presence with a pin. These details are in the lines.

But then Lear suggests a reconciliation between daughter and father. The question is how best to show this reconciliation and how best to show its religious overtones? Lear *must* kneel to Cordelia. It is in the script. However the scene can be made more moving if Cordelia also kneels and so we have the picture of a reunion based on humility—two people kneeling and asking each other for forgiveness. One problem is to decide when Cordelia kneels.

What other movements and actions are possible to make the scene one that "enriches the feelings"?

The following passage describes how some actors have played the scene as Lear:

Devrient only clasped his hands, as if he prayed that he saw aright; and Gielgud, his voice full of love, flung out his hands to Cordelia, who knelt to him, seized the hands, and caressed them. Mantell reached out to stroke Cordelia's hair—but could not look her in the face. Classically this has been an opportunity for Lear to take Cordelia in his arms: so Salvini's fatherly embrace.

M. Rosenberg, *The Masks of King Lear*

What other possibilities can you see?

King Lear 2 (Act V, Scene III)
Lear and Cordelia are reunited but they are imprisoned by their enemies. While in prison Cordelia is hanged. In the following scene we see the former king, the father who has been cruel and selfish, with his beloved daughter. He grabs at any chance that she may still be alive. Edgar and Kent are friends of Lear.

[Enter Lear with Cordelia in his arms; followed by gentleman]

LEAR: Howl, howl, howl! Oh you are men of stones.
    Had I your tongues and eyes, I'd use them so
    That heaven's vault should crack. She's gone for ever.
    I know when one is dead, and when one lives:
    She's dead as earth. Lend me a looking-glass:

23

If that her breath will mist or stain the stone,
Why then she lives.

KENT: Is this the promis'd end?

EDGAR: Or image of that horror?

ALBANY: Fall and cease. 10

LEAR: This feather stirs—she lives! If it be so,
It is a chance which does redeem all sorrows
That ever I have felt.

KENT: O my good master—

LEAR: Prithee away.

EDGAR: 'Tis noble Kent, your friend.

LEAR: A plague upon you, murderers, traitors all!
I might have sav'd her; now she's gone for ever!
Cordelia, Cordelia, stay a little. Ha!
What is't thou say'st? Her voice was ever soft, 20
Gentle and low, an excellent thing in woman.
I kill'd the slave that was a-hanging thee.

GENTLEMAN: 'Tis true, my lords, he did.

LEAR: Did I not, fellow?
I have seen the day, with my good biting falchion
I would have made him skip. I am old now,
And these same crosses spoil me. Who are you?
Mine eyes are not o' th' best, I'll tell you straight.

KENT: If Fortune brag of two she lov'd and hated,
One of them we behold. 30

LEAR: This is a dull sight. Are you not Kent?

KENT: The same—
Your servant Kent. Where is your servant Caius?

LEAR: He's a good fellow, I can tell you that:
He'll strike, and quickly too. He's dead and rotten.

KENT: No, my good lord, I am the very man—

LEAR: I'll see that straight.

KENT: That from your first of difference and decay
Have follow'd your sad steps—

LEAR: You are welcome hither. 40

KENT: Nor no man else. All's cheerless, dark and deadly.
Your eldest daughters have fordone themselves,
And desperately are dead.

LEAR: Ay, so I think.

ALBANY: He knows not what he says, and vain it is
That we present us to him.

EDGAR: Very bootless.

[Enter a messenger]

MESSENGER: Edmund is dead, my lord.

ALBANY: That's but a trifle here.
You lords and noble friends, know our intent: 50
What comfort to this great decay may come

24

Shall be appli'd. For us, we will resign,
During the life of this old majesty,
To him our absolute power.
[*To Edgar and Kent*] You to your rights,
With boot, and such addition as your honours
Have more than merited. All friends shall taste
The wages of their virtue, and all foes
The cup of their deservings—Oh see, see!

LEAR: And my poor fool is hang'd. No, no, no life! 60
Why should a dog, a horse, a rat, have life,
And thou no breath at all? Thou'lt come no more,
Never, never, never, never, never.
Pray you, undo this button. Thank you, sir.
Do you see this? Look on her! Look, her lips—
Look there, look there!

[He dies]

EDGAR: He faints. My lord, my lord!
KENT: Break, heart; I prithee break!
EDGAR: Look up, my lord.
KENT: Vex not his ghost. Oh let him pass. He hates him 70
That would upon the rack of this tough world
Stretch him out longer.

There are some lines in the text that require actions. For example, Lear
must ask for a looking-glass; he must undo the button on his jacket. Can
you find others?

This has been called one of the most moving scenes in Shakespeare. What
small actions can add to the pathos?

For example:

• Where does Lear find the feather to test whether Cordelia lives? One actor
demanded a feather from Kent; another plucked a plume from a soldier's
helmet; another used a wisp of Cordelia's hair.

• How does Lear die? Does he die in joy thinking Cordelia lives; does he
die shocked by the sight of Cordelia's lifeless body; does he die quietly
in his grief; does he die pumping at Cordelia's heart, holding her close?
Your answers to any of these questions will influence your decision as to
how Lear dies.

PHYSICAL BEARING AND MOVEMENT

Movement, gesture and physical appearance are powerful means of expression. They are a form of language and can enrich the interchanges of speech as well as illustrate the inner responses and feelings of the characters. These are the main elements:

- Using different attitudes. For example, someone may be sitting in a dejected manner. He suddenly makes a decision; he stands upright and moves to a more commanding position.
- Turning and walking. New thoughts or new emotions can dictate the turning of the body. For example, a commander in a tense situation may become more and more angry as he moves around a desk giving orders.
- Gesture can enhance the meaning of a scene. A hand placed on the shoulder of a person can show friendship. The length of time it is left there can significantly alter the tone of the movement.
- Facial expression can reveal emotions. For example, picture the situation after there has been a very savage family row. The family sits down to the tea table. Each person's facial expression and posture reveal the rôle he or she has played in the row.

Exercises

1. Practise other small scenes which illustrate the above elements. Do not use words. Classmates should try to guess what has happened in the scene.
    - You are waiting for a very important phone call. Your nerves are on edge. The phone rings.
    - A woman who is a secret drinker visits friends. Finding no one at home she explores the small flat, searching for liquor. She takes a drink to quieten her nerves.
    - Students enter the acting space and convey only by gesture and movement as much information as they can about who they are, and where they have come from. The rest of the class guesses the details. (It might be useful to try this exercise with any of the Shakespearean characters in this book.)

Merchant of Venice 1 (Act III, Scene I)
Shylock, a Jew, is a usurer who has made an immense fortune by lending money to Christians at a high interest. His greatest enemy is Antonio, a wealthy businessman. Antonio needs money to lend to a friend and goes to Shylock to borrow it. Shylock agrees to lend the money but under strange conditions: if Antonio does not repay it by a certain day he forfeits to Shylock a pound of his flesh. In this scene Shylock is raging against Antonio. Why does he feel this intense hatred? Antonio lends money without interest; hating the Jews and their faith, he has abused Shylock, and with his friends has helped Shylock's daughter to run away and marry a Christian.

SHYLOCK: Let him look to his bond. He was wont to call me usurer.
Let him look to his bond. He was wont to lend money
for a Christian courtesy. Let him look to his bond.

SALERIO: Why, I am sure if he forfeit thou wilt not take his
    flesh. What's that good for?
SHYLOCK: To bait fish withal. If it will feed nothing else,
    it will feed my revenge. He hath disgraced me and hindered
    me half a million, laughed at my losses, mocked at
    my gains, scorned my nation, thwarted my bargains,
    cooled my friends, heated mine enemies, and what's his   10
    reason? I am a Jew. Hath not a Jew eyes? Hath not a
    Jew hands, organs, dimensions, senses, affections, passions?
    Fed with the same food, hurt with the same
    weapons, subject to the same diseases, healed by the
    same means, warmed and cooled by the same winter and
    summer as a Christian is? If you prick us, do we not
    bleed? If you tickle us, do we not laugh? If you poison
    us, do we not die? And if you wrong us, shall we not
    revenge? If we are like you in the rest, we will resemble
    you in that. If a Jew wrong a Christian, what is his   20
    humility? Revenge. If a Christian wrong a Jew, what
    should his sufferance be by Christian example? Why,
    revenge! The villainy you teach me I will execute, and it
    shall go hard but I will better the instruction.

It is quite possible to play this scene in two ways:
- Shylock can be played as a brooding, evil villain. He is a distorted man full
  of petty jealousies and intense hatred. His appearance and his crouching
  posture remind us of a dangerous animal. He whispers the lines with a
  cold ferocity and his words are accompanied by short, violent actions as
  his eyes blaze ferocious hate.
- Shylock can be played as a tragic hero. He is suffering intensely but there
  is forbearance in his pain. Although there is a ferocity in his speech, he
  stands erect and moves with dignity. He is a man we admire as we sorrow
  for him and for his race. This is not a pathetic or a monstrous Jew. He is
  a man who calls for justice, and he makes the call calmly and proudly.

Merchant of Venice 2 (Act IV, Scene I)
Antonio has received news that his ships have been lost. The day of payment
being past, Shylock insists on having a pound of Antonio's flesh. Following
is part of the trial scene. Portia is defending Antonio. She calls for mercy;
he refuses. Antonio's friends offer the money, and more; he refuses. Portia
says nothing can be done. Shylock is triumphant, but his victory is short-
lived.

PORTIA: Why then, thus it is:
    You must prepare your bosom for his knife.
SHYLOCK: O noble judge! O excellent young man!
PORTIA: For the intent and purpose of the law
    Hath full relation to the penalty,
    Which here appeareth due upon the bond.

SHYLOCK: 'Tis very true. O wise and upright judge!
How much more elder art thou than thy looks!
PORTIA: Therefore lay bare your bosom.
SHYLOCK: Ay, his breast,   10
So says the bond, doth it not, noble judge?
"Nearest his heart", those are the very words.
PORTIA: It is so. Are there balance here to weigh
The flesh?
SHYLOCK: I have them ready.
PORTIA: Have by some surgeon, Shylock, on your charge,
To stop his wounds, lest he do bleed to death.
SHYLOCK: Is it so nominated in the bond?
PORTIA: It is not so expressed, but what of that?
'Twere good you do so much for charity.   20
SHYLOCK: I cannot find it; 'tis not in the bond.
PORTIA: A pound of that same merchant's flesh is thine,
The court awards it, and the law doth give it.
SHYLOCK: Most rightful judge!
PORTIA: And you must cut this flesh from off his breast,
The law allows it, and the court awards it.
SHYLOCK: Most learned judge! A sentence! Come, prepare!
PORTIA: Tarry a little, there is something else.
This bond doth give thee here no jot of blood;
The words expressly are "a pound of flesh".   30
Take then thy bond, take thou thy pound of flesh,
But in the cutting it if thou dost shed
One drop of Christian blood, thy lands and goods
Are by the laws of Venice confiscate
Unto the state of Venice.
GRATIANO: O upright judge! Mark, Jew. O learned judge!
SHYLOCK: Is that the law?
PORTIA: Thyself shalt see the act,
For, as thou urgest justice, be assured
Thou shalt have justice more than thou desir'st.   40
GRATIANO: O learned judge! Mark, Jew. A learned judge!
SHYLOCK: I take this offer then. Pay the bond thrice
And let the Christian go.
BASSANIO: Here is the money.
PORTIA: Soft!
The Jew shall have all justice. Soft, no haste,
He shall have nothing but the penalty.
GRATIANO: O Jew! An upright judge, a learned judge!
PORTIA: Therefore prepare thee to cut off the flesh.
Shed thou no blood, nor cut thou less nor more   50
But just a pound of flesh. If thou tak'st more
Or less than a just pound, be it but so much
As makes it light or heavy in the substance
Or the division of the twentieth part

28

Of one poor scruple, nay, if the scale do turn
But in the estimation of a hair,
Thou diest, and all thy goods are confiscate.
GRATIANO: A second Daniel! A Daniel, Jew!
Now, infidel, I have you on the hip!
PORTIA: Why doth the Jew pause? Take thy forfeiture.   60
SHYLOCK: Give me my principal, and let me go.
BASSANIO: I have it ready for thee; here it is.
PORTIA: He hath refused it in the open court.
He shall have merely justice and his bond.
GRATIANO: A Daniel still say I, a second Daniel!
I thank thee, Jew, for teaching me that word.
SHYLOCK: Shall I not have barely my principal?
PORTIA: Thou shalt have nothing but the forfeiture,
To be so taken at thy peril, Jew.
SHYLOCK: Why, then the devil give him good of it!   70
I'll stay no longer question.
PORTIA: Tarry, Jew!
The law hath yet another hold on you.
It is enacted in the laws of Venice,
If it be proved against an alien
That by direct or indirect attempts
He seek the life of any citizen,
The party 'gainst the which he doth contrive
Shall seize one half his goods, the other half
Comes to the privy coffer of the state,   80
And the offender's life lies in the mercy
Of the Duke only, 'gainst all other voice,
In which predicament I say thou stand'st,
For it appears by manifest proceeding
That indirectly, and directly too,
Thou hast contrived against the very life
Of the defendant, and thou hast incurred
The danger formerly by me rehearsed.
Down therefore, and beg mercy of the Duke.
GRATIANO: Beg that thou mayst have leave to hang thyself,   90
And yet, thy wealth, being forfeit to the state,
Thou hast not left the value of a cord,
Therefore thou must be hanged at the state's charge.
DUKE: That thou shalt see the difference of our spirit,
I pardon thee thy life before thou ask it.
For half thy wealth, it is Antonio's,
The other half comes to the general state,
Which humbleness may drive unto a fine.
PORTIA: Ay, for the state, not for Antonio.
SHYLOCK: Nay, take my life and all! Pardon not that!   100
You take my house when you do take the prop
That doth sustain my house. You take my life

29

When you do take the means whereby I live.

PORTIA: What mercy can you render him, Antonio?

GRATIANO: A halter gratis! Nothing else, for God's sake!

ANTONIO: So please my lord the Duke and all the court
To quit the fine for one half of his goods,
I am content, so he will let me have
The other half in use, to render it
Upon his death unto the gentleman   110
That lately stole his daughter.
Two things provided more: that for this favour
He presently become a Christian;
The other, that he do record a gift
Here in the court of all he dies possessed
Unto his son Lorenzo and his daughter.

DUKE: He shall do this, or else I do recant
The pardon that I late pronouncèd here.

PORTIA: Art thou contented, Jew? What dost thou say?

SHYLOCK: I am content.   120

PORTIA: Clerk, draw a deed of gift.

SHYLOCK: I pray you give me leave to go from hence,
I am not well; send the deed after me,
And I will sign it.

DUKE: Get thee gone, but do it.

GRATIANO: In christ'ning shalt thou have two godfathers.
Had I been judge, thou shouldst have had ten more,
To bring thee to the gallows, not to the font.

[Exit Shylock]

Draw a stage design of the court. Where you place Portia, Shylock and Antonio, where the knife and scales are, and where entrances are to be made will all influence the movements in the scene.

There are many clues to movement in the text. How many can you find? A good technique is to use some object to represent each character. Each figure has its own reader and mover.

Say "I am content" resentfully, sarcastically, humbly. Your posture, gesture, and facial expression will be influenced by the way you say the lines.

The fortunes of each side change during the scene. How will these changes in fortune influence the physical bearing and movements of the characters?

Have different class members perform Shylock's exit. After discussing the various attempts, examine the following description of the scene:

And there is yet the silence in which Shylock leaves, hearing the Duke's curt command and Gratiano's jibe; this cannot fail to impress the audience, at least with his physical weakness, as he moves slowly and with difficulty, and probably with his restraint and isolation in saying nothing more; and if he turns towards Gratiano for a moment only, there will be an impression of rekindled scorn for such Christians, or of now-impotent hatred.

John Russell Brown, *Shakespeare's Plays in Performance*

CROWDS, ENTRANCES, EXITS

Crowd scenes must be built up and controlled carefully. An important factor in the building up is the control of exits and entrances: these can point to significances of situation, suggest mood, and show character and character relationships. For example:

- A succession of quick entrances can announce danger and excitement.
- One or more quiet entrances can build up a sense of tension.
- A noisy crowd exiting leaving one person alone can make a useful contrast.

Exercises

1. Make an entrance which suggests a mood: sadness, fear, expectation, resignation, gaiety.
2. Make an exit which suggests a similar mood.
3. Students take one or more of the Shakespearean characters in this book and perform an entrance or exit for the character(s). The rest of the class guesses who the character(s) is (are).
4. There is a busy but relaxed street scene. Each person takes up a character: the barber standing outside his shop, the mother entering with a pram, a young man waiting outside a phone box et cetera. Build up this scene. A plane comes over and strafes the street. Use a sound instrument to denote the strafing. What happens next? Work on the following:
   - How to convey that it is a pleasant relaxed street.
   - How to show various relationships between the people.
   - How to show that you are in character.
   - How to emphasise the contrast between the early scene and the scene after strafing.

Romeo and Juliet 1 (Act I, Scene I)

There are two rival houses in Verona, the Montagues and the Capulets. In the opening scene the servants of the two houses skirmish with each other in the public square. Because the two families are ancient enemies, the servants feel obliged to confront each other whenever they meet. The servants are an uneducated lot, not dangerous and not very courageous. Their object is to insult and carry out minor physical assaults. Sampson and Gregory are servants to Capulet; Abraham and Balthasar servants to Montague. Benvolio is a nephew of Montague, and Tybalt a nephew of Capulet. The latter two are both courageous and dangerous.

GREGORY: Draw thy tool, here comes two of the house of Montagues.

[Enter two other serving-men, Abraham and Balthasar]

SAMPSON: My naked weapon is out. Quarrel, I will back thee.

GREGORY: How, turn thy back and run?

SAMPSON: Fear me not.

GREGORY: No marry, I fear thee!

SAMPSON: Let us take the law of our sides, let them begin.

GREGORY: I will frown as I pass by, and let them take it as they list.

SAMPSON: Nay, as they dare. I will bite my thumb at them, which is disgrace to them if they bear it.

ABRAHAM: Do you bite your thumb at us sir?　　　　　　　　　　　10

SAMPSON: I do bite my thumb sir.

ABRAHAM: Do you bite your thumb at us sir?

SAMPSON: *[Aside to Gregory]* Is the law of our side if I say "Ay"?

GREGORY: *[Aside to Sampson]* No.

SAMPSON: No sir, I do not bite my thumb at you sir, but I bite my thumb sir.

GREGORY: Do you quarrel sir?

ABRAHAM: Quarrel sir? No sir.

SAMPSON: But if you do sir, I am for you. I serve as good a man as you.

ABRAHAM: No better.

SAMPSON: Well sir.　　　　　　　　　　　　　　　　　　　20

[Enter Benvolio]

GREGORY: *[Aside to Sampson]* Say "better"; here comes one of my master's kinsmen.

SAMPSON: Yes, better sir.

ABRAHAM: You lie.

SAMPSON: Draw if you be men. Gregory, remember thy washing blow.

[They fight]

BENVOLIO: Part fools.
　　　Put up your swords, you know not what you do.

[Enter Tybalt]

TYBALT: What, are thou drawn among these heartless hinds?
　　　Turn thee Benvolio, look upon thy death.

BENVOLIO: I do but keep the peace. Put up thy sword,
　　　Or manage it to part these men with me.　　　　　　30

TYBALT: What, drawn and talk of peace? I hate the word,
　　　As I hate hell, all Montagues, and thee.
　　　Have at thee coward!

[They fight. Enter Officer and Citizens with clubs and partisans]

OFFICER: Clubs, bills, and partisans! Strike, beat them down.
　　　Down with the Capulets! Down with the Montagues!

[Enter old Capulet in his gown, and Lady Capulet]

CAPULET: What noise is this? Give me my long sword, ho!

LADY CAPULET: A crutch, a crutch! Why call you for a sword?

CAPULET: My sword I say! Old Montague is come,
　　　And flourishes his blade in spite of me.

[Enter old Montague and Lady Montague]

MONTAGUE: Thou villain Capulet! Hold me not, let me go.　　　40

LADY MONTAGUE: Thou shalt not stir one foot to seek a foe.

[Enter Prince Escalus, with his train]

PRINCE: Rebellious subjects, enemies to peace,
          Profaners of this neighbour-stained steel—
          Will they not hear?—What ho! You men, you beasts,
          That quench the fire of your pernicious rage
          With purple fountains issuing from your veins,
          On pain of torture, from those bloody hands
          Throw your mistempered weapons to the ground,
          And hear the sentence of your moved Prince.
          Three civil brawls bred of an airy word,   50
          By thee old Capulet, and Montague,
          Have thrice disturbed the quiet of our streets,
          And made Verona's ancient citizens
          Cast by their grave beseeming ornaments,
          To wield old partisans, in hands as old,
          Cankered with peace, to part your cankered hate.
          If ever you disturb our streets again,
          Your lives shall pay the forfeit of the peace.
          For this time all the rest depart away.
          You Capulet shall go along with me.   60
          And Montague, come you this afternoon,
          To know our further pleasure in this case,
          To old Freetown, our common judgement-place.
          Once more, on pain of death, all men depart.

                          [Exeunt]

   In this scene we have to introduce the characters in successive entrances
and what starts as a small and childish skirmish builds up into a confrontation
suggesting serious danger.
   We need a quiet opening with the clownish Sampson and Gregory rather
nervously looking for a fight. Their first lines should be whispered as they
see Balthasar and Abraham enter in the distance. This silly banter continues
into a mock fight until the vicious Tybalt enters and talks of death and means
it. This new note of violence builds with the arrival of more citizens. They
enter shouting, and harsh words lash out. Before long the stage is full of
duelling figures. The entrance of the Prince must be dignified and formal and
his speech measured to contrast with the scene he interrupts.
   It is important that each successive entrance be quicker than the last, to
correspond with the more agitated, violent language.
   The Prince's speech is followed by a complete silence. Each exit is
performed in this silence. It would be useful to work out in what order each
character moves off and in what direction.
   Following is how one drama critic sees the scene. Work on his ideas and
decide if you agree with him.

   Notice how the entrances are built up: servants, gentlemen, lords, and the
Prince, in order. He enters from a platform and speaks first from its central
steps; the noise dwindles, then rises. The fighting has stopped. He carves
a way down centre, the officers pushing people aside. There are still

murmurs. He is right down to the words "Throw your mistempered weapons to the ground". There is complete silence. A pause. Then, "And hear the sentence of your moved Prince". He turns—the deliberate throwing away of stage presence by a turn up-stage underlines his absolute authority—and walks up-stage, followed by the officers. Standing on the steps he speaks the rest, officers either side, the whole group, who have had time to get to new positions, listening: many have their backs half-turned to the audience, giving extra emphasis to the Prince's importance.

G. Wilson Knight, *Principles of Shakespearean Production*

Romeo and Juliet 2 (Act III, Scene I)
At this stage Romeo (a Montague) has fallen in love with Juliet (a Capulet). Mercutio, a friend of Romeo, meets with Tybalt, a cousin of Juliet. They fight and Mercutio is wounded. Tybalt runs away but a few seconds later returns and fights with Romeo. Tybalt is killed.

[Enter Tybalt, Petruchio, and others]

BENVOLIO: By my head, here comes the Capulets.
MERCUTIO: By my heel, I care not.
TYBALT: Follow me close, for I will speak to them.
    Gentlemen, good den; a word with one of you.
MERCUTIO: And but one word with one of us? Couple it with
    something, make it a word and a blow.
TYBALT: You shall find me apt enough to that sir, an you will
    give me occasion.
MERCUTIO: Could you not take some occasion without giving?
TYBALT: Mercutio, thou consortest with Romeo.
MERCUTIO: Consort? What, dost thou make us minstrels? An   10
    thou make minstrels of us, look to hear nothing but discords.
    Here's my fiddlestick, here's that shall make you dance.
    'Zounds, consort!
BENVOLIO: We talk here in the public haunt of men.
    Either withdraw into some private place,
    And reason coldly of your grievances,
    Or else depart; here all eyes gaze on us.
MERCUTIO: Men's eyes were made to look, and let them gaze.
    I will not budge for no man's pleasure, I.

[Enter Romeo]

TYBALT: Well, peace be with you sir, here comes my man.   20
MERCUTIO: But I'll be hanged sir, if he wear your livery.
    Marry go before to field, he'll be your follower;
    Your worship in that sense may call him man.
TYBALT: Romeo, the love I bear thee can afford
    No better term than this—thou art a villain.
ROMEO: Tybalt, the reason that I have to love thee
    Doth much excuse the appertaining rage
    To such a greeting. Villain am I none.

Therefore farewell, I see thou knowest me not.

TYBALT: Boy, this shall not excuse the injuries   30
    That thou hast done me, therefore turn and draw.

ROMEO: I do protest I never injuried thee,
    But love thee better than thou canst devise,
    Till thou shalt know the reason of my love.
    And so good Capulet, which name I tender
    As dearly as my own, be satisfied.

MERCUTIO: O calm, dishonourable, vile submission!
    Alla stoccata carries it away.
    Tybalt, you rat-catcher, will you walk?

TYBALT: What wouldst thou have with me?   40

MERCUTIO: Good King of Cats, nothing but one of your nine
    lives, that I mean to make bold withal, and as you shall use me
    hereafter, dry-beat the rest of the eight. Will you pluck your
    sword out of his pilcher by the ears? Make haste, lest mine be
    about your ears ere it be out.

TYBALT: I am for you.

ROMEO: Gentle Mercutio, put thy rapier up.

MERCUTIO: Come sir, your *passado*.

ROMEO: Draw Benvolio, beat down their weapons.
    Gentlemen, for shame, forbear this outrage.   50
    Tybalt, Mercutio, the Prince expressly hath
    Forbid this bandying in Verona streets.
    Hold Tybalt. Good Mercutio.

PETRUCHIO: Away Tybalt. "*Tybalt under Romeo's arm, thrusts
    Mercutio in and flies*"

MERCUTIO: I am hurt.
    A plague on both your houses, I am sped.
    Is he gone and hath nothing?

BENVOLIO: What, art thou hurt?

MERCUTIO: Ay, ay, a scratch, a scratch; marry 'tis enough.
    Where is my page? Go villain, fetch a surgeon.   60

[Exit Page]

ROMEO: Courage man, the hurt cannot be much.

MERCUTIO: No 'tis not so deep as a well, nor so wide as a
    church-door; but 'tis enough, 'twill serve. Ask for me tomorrow,
    and you shall find me a grave man. I am peppered, I
    warrant, for this world. A plague on both your houses!
    'Zounds, a dog, a rat, a mouse, a cat, to scratch a man to death!
    A braggart, a rogue, a villain, that fights by the book of
    arithmetic! Why the devil came you between us? I was hurt
    under your arm.

ROMEO: I thought all for the best.

MERCUTIO: Help me into some house Benvolio,   70
    Or I shall faint. A plague a'both your houses!
    They have made worms' meat of me. I have it,

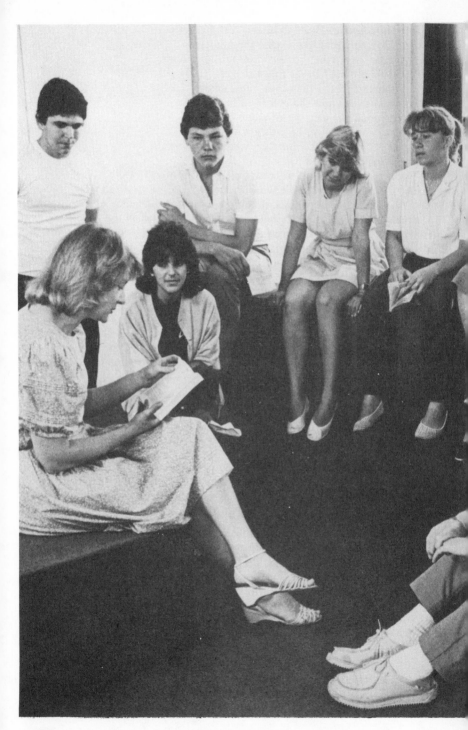

And soundly too. Your houses!

[Exeunt Mercutio and Benvolio]

ROMEO: This gentleman, the Prince's near ally,
My very friend, hath got this mortal hurt
In my behalf; my reputation stained
With Tybalt's slander. Tybalt that an hour
Hath been my cousin. O sweet Juliet,
Thy beauty hath made me effeminate,
And in my temper softened valour's steel.   80

[Enter Benvolio]

BENVOLIO: O Romeo, Romeo, brave Mercutio is dead.
That gallant spirit hath aspired the clouds,
Which too untimely here did scorn the earth.
ROMEO: This day's black fate on moe days doth depend,
This but begins the woe others must end.

[Enter Tybalt]

BENVOLIO: Here comes the furious Tybalt back again.
ROMEO: He go in triumph, and Mercutio slain?
Away to heaven respective lenity,
And fire-eyed fury be my conduct now.
Now Tybalt take the "villain" back again   90
That late thou gavest me, for Mercutio's soul
Is but a little way above our heads,
Staying for thine to keep him company.
Either thou or I, or both, must go with him.
TYBALT: Thou wretched boy, that didst consort him here,
Shalt with him hence.
ROMEO: This shall determine that.

[They fight. Tybalt falls]

BENVOLIO: Romeo away, be gone.
The citizens are up, and Tybalt slain.
Stand not amazed, the Prince will doom thee death,   100
If thou art taken. Hence, be gone, away.
ROMEO: O I am fortune's fool!
BENVOLIO: Why dost thou stay?

[Exit Romeo. Enter Citizens]

CITIZEN: Which way ran he that killed Mercutio?
Tybalt, that murderer, which way ran he?
BENVOLIO: There lies that Tybalt.
CITIZEN: Up sir, go with me;
I charge thee in the Prince's name obey.

[Enter Prince, Montague, Capulet, their Wives and all]

PRINCE: Where are the vile beginners of this fray?
BENVOLIO: O noble Prince, I can discover all   110

The unlucky manage of this fatal brawl.
There lies the man, slain by young Romeo,
That slew thy kinsman, brave Mercutio.
LADY CAPULET: Tybalt, my cousin. O my brother's child!
O Prince! O husband! O the blood is spilled
Of my dear kinsman! Prince, as thou art true,
For blood of ours shed blood of Montague.
O cousin, cousin!
PRINCE: Romeo slew him, he slew Mercutio.
Who now the price of his dear blood doth owe?   120
MONTAGUE: Not Romeo, Prince, he was Mercutio's friend;
His fault concludes but what the law should end,
The life of Tybalt.
PRINCE: And for that offence
Immediately we do exile him hence.
I have an interest in your hate's proceeding;
My blood for your rude brawls doth lie a-bleeding.
But I'll amerce you with so strong a fine,
That you shall all repent the loss of mine.
I will be deaf to pleading and excuses,   130
Nor tears nor prayers shall purchase out abuses.
Therefore use none. Let Romeo hence in haste,
Else, when he's found, that hour is his last.
Bear hence this body, and attend our will.
Mercy but murders, pardoning those that kill.

[Exeunt. Enter Juliet]

Make your own model theatre on the desk. Have a number of objects (chessmen are ideal) representing each character. These objects are then set up and made to meet each other as the text requires. Speak aloud the lines of each character as he or she is moved.

Rehearse the building up of this scene. The following points on entrances and exits may help.
• Mercutio is on stage relaxing and joking.
• Tybalt enters looking for violence. Does he immediately go up to Mercutio?
• Romeo enters, his mind only on his love for Juliet. How can his entrance show his lack of awareness of the danger?
• Mercutio is badly injured. Would a silence on stage, as Romeo watches Mercutio wounded and Tybalt rushes off, help?
• The furious Tybalt returns. How can the entrance of Tybalt be made full of suspense?
• An excited crowd enters.
• The stage empties and leaves one figure, Juliet, who has wandered on unaware of what has happened.

Discuss the following comment on this scene:

Since the plays were performed without break, the balancing of crowd against single figure also works from scene to scene. In *Romeo and*

Juliet, the scene of the death of Mercutio and Tybalt is towards its end crowded and excited, all Verona seems to be on stage . . .

As the stage empties, the one person unaware of events or of her lover's banishment appears . . . The effect of change from the crowd to the individual has the additional value of showing the audience that Juliet faces the world alone.

J. L. Styan, Shakespeare's Stagecraft

Section Two
Sub-text in Scenes Grouped Thematically

Valuable as the exercise is, it is artificial to look at each of the elements of the sub-text in isolation. This section groups scenes under thematic headings. On the left hand page, instead of the usual scholarly information, are included ideas and questions related to all the elements to encourage discussion and performance.

CROWD SCENES

Grouping for the scene is difficult because there are so many characters and at times it is difficult to see who is speaking to whom. There are several stage movements necessary for the characters.

Draw a stage diagram and by the use of arrows show when and where the characters move. Then practise stepping out the scene testing the ideas in your diagrams.

What evidence is there at the beginning to show that the conspirators are in a state of intense nervous excitement?

Practise different readings of Caesar's speeches—first loud, then quietly, slowly, then fast, high pitch followed by low pitch. It is useful to practise your readings into a tape recorder; as you play the tape back new meanings and effects will become more apparent.

Practise reading Caesar's speeches:
• showing Caesar as a man full of his own bombast.
• reading them with the rhythm and diction of greatness.

Julius Caesar has become very powerful in Rome. There are various people who are opposed to him. They have different reasons for their opposition: Brutus is against the idea of kingship in Rome; Cassius' reasons are more personal; he is jealous of Caesar's power. A number of conspirators, led by Brutus and Cassius, plan to murder Caesar.

[A crowd of people; among them Artemidorus and the Soothsayer. Flourish. Enter Caesar, Brutus, Cassius, Casca, Decius, Metellus, Trebonius, Cinna, Antony, Lepidus, Popilius, Publius, and others]

POPILIUS: I wish your enterprise today may thrive.
CASSIUS: What enterprise Popilius?
POPILIUS: Fare you well.
BRUTUS: What said Popilius Lena?
CASSIUS: He wished today our enterprise might thrive.
    I fear our purpose is discovered.
BRUTUS: Look how he makes to Caesar. Mark him.
CASSIUS: Casca, be sudden, for we fear prevention.
    Brutus, what shall be done? If this be known,
    Cassius or Caesar never shall turn back,   10
    For I will slay myself.

BRUTUS: Cassius be constant.
    Popilius Lena speaks not of our purposes,
    For look, he smiles, and Caesar doth not change.
CASSIUS: Trebonius knows his time; for look you Brutus,
    He draws Mark Antony out of the way.

[Exeunt Antony and Trebonius]

DECIUS: Where is Metellus Cimber? Let him go,
    And presently prefer his suit to Caesar.
BRUTUS: He is addressed; press near and second him.
CINNA: Casca, you are the first that rears your hand.   20
CAESAR: Are we all ready? What is now amiss
    That Caesar and his senate must redress?
METELLUS: Most high, most mighty, and most puissant Caesar,
    Metellus Cimber throws before thy seat
    An humble heart.

[Kneeling]

CAESAR: I must prevent thee Cimber.
    These couchings, and these lowly courtesies
    Might fire the blood of ordinary men,
    And turn pre-ordinance and first decree
    Into the law of children. Be not fond,   30
    To think that Caesar bears such rebel blood
    That will be thawed from the true quality
    With that which melteth fools; I mean sweet words,
    Low-crooked curtsies, and base spaniel fawning.

The killing of Caesar. Shakespeare gives very simple stage directions: "They stab Caesar". How does a director arrange an effective and dramatic killing? Points to consider:

- How would each conspirator react in the stabbing? You would have to consider the mental state of each as he stabs Caesar. Some of the lines will give you some clues.
- The physical process of the stabbing will have to be worked on. From which direction does each conspirator come? How many times do they stab? In what order? Doing the first attempts in slow motion may help here.
- How should Brutus kill Caesar? Would the fact that Brutus loves Caesar and is killing him for the good of Rome, whereas the others hate him and are killing him for more personal reasons, influence your decision?

One group of students suggested the following possibilities:
- As the conspirators hack away at Caesar, Brutus, who has been standing aside, moves forward and ceremonially stabs him.
- Caesar, as he is dying, moves towards his friend for protection. They claimed this added greater pathos to Caesar's line: *"Et tu Brute."* Practise both suggestions and decide which is the more effective. Are there any other possibilites?

CASCA: Speak hands for me!

Thy brother by decree is banished.
If thou dost bend, and pray, and fawn for him,
I spurn thee like a cur out of my way.
Know, Caesar doth not wrong, nor without cause
Will he be satisfied.

METELLUS: Is there no voice more worthy than my own,   40
To sound more sweetly in great Caesar's ear
For the repealing of my banished brother?

BRUTUS: I kiss thy hand, but not in flattery Caesar;
Desiring thee that Publius Cimber may
Have an immediate freedom of repeal.

CAESAR: What, Brutus?

CASSIUS: Pardon Caesar; Caesar, pardon:
As low as to thy foot doth Cassius fall,
To beg enfranchisement for Publius Cimber.

CAESAR: I could be well moved, if I were as you;   50
If I could pray to move, prayers would move me.
But I am constant as the northern star,
Of whose true-fixed and resting quality
There is no fellow in the firmament.
The skies are painted with unnumbered sparks,
They are all fire, and every one doth shine;
But there's but one in all doth hold his place.
So in the world; 'tis furnished well with men,
And men are flesh and blood, and apprehensive;
Yet in the number I do know but one   60
That unassailable holds on his rank,
Unshaked of motion; and that I am he,
Let me a little show it, even in this,
That I was constant Cimber should be banished,
And constant do remain to keep him so.

CINNA: O Caesar—

CAESAR: Hence! Wilt thou lift up Olympus?

DECIUS: Great Caesar—

CAESAR: Doth not Brutus bootless kneel?   70

CASCA: Speak hands for me!

[They stab Caesar]

CAESAR: *Et tu Brute?* Then fall Caesar!

[Dies]

Julius Caesar 2 (Act III, Scene II)
Brutus and Antony go to the Forum to explain to an unruly, ill-educated crowd
why Caesar has been killed. We already know that Antony is going to use
the opportunity to turn the crowd against the conspirators. But how is he
going to do it? His task is made more difficult as Brutus speaks first and
wins the crowd over.

Experiment with two ways of reading Brutus' speech:
- Read it with as little movement as possible, using only one physical attitude for the entire speech.
- Divide the speech into its main parts and select a movement, gesture and physical attitude appropriate to each. Decide whether the tone will change for each section.

Brutus stands almost helpless in the tumult he has caused. Take the broken line "My countrymen—": does he feel that the citizens are going too far? Would he say it in a tone of criticism? Or does he approve of the behaviour but feel incapable of controlling it?

A character who is spatially separated from the group and who is silent as well can have a special strength. How can Antony's entrance and position during Brutus' speech show he is an ominous figure?

THIRD CITIZEN: The noble Brutus is ascended. Silence!

BRUTUS: Be patient till the last.

Romans, countrymen, and lovers, hear me for my cause, and be silent, that you may hear. Believe me for mine honour, and have respect to mine honour, that you may believe. Censure me in your wisdom, and awake your senses, that you may the better judge. If there be any in this assembly, any dear friend of Caesar's, to him I say, that Brutus' love to Caesar was no less than his. If then that friend demand why Brutus rose against Caesar, this is my answer—not that I loved Caesar less, but that I loved Rome more. Had you rather Caesar were living, and die all slaves, than that Caesar were dead, to live all free men? As Caesar loved me, I weep for him; as he was fortunate, I rejoice at it; as he was valiant, I honour him; but as he was ambitious, I slew him. There is tears, for his love; joy, for his fortune; honour, for his valour; and death, for his ambition. Who is here so base, that would be a bondman? If any, speak, for him have I offended. Who is here so rude that would not be a Roman? If any, speak, for him have I offended. Who is here so vile that will not love his country? If any, speak, for him have I offended. I pause for a reply.

ALL: None Brutus, none.

BRUTUS: Then none have I offended. I have done no more to Caesar than you shall do to Brutus. The question of his death is enrolled in the Capitol; his glory not extenuated, wherein he was worthy; nor his offences enforced, for which he suffered death.

[Enter Antony with Caesar's body]

Here comes his body, mourned by Mark Antony, who though he had no hand in his death, shall receive the benefit of his dying, a place in the commonwealth, as which of you shall not? With this I depart, that as I slew my best lover for the good of Rome, I have the same dagger for myself, when it shall please my country to need my death.

ALL: Live Brutus, live, live!

FIRST CITIZEN: Bring him with triumph home unto his house.

SECOND CITIZEN: Give him a statue with his ancestors.

THIRD CITIZEN: Let him be Caesar.

FOURTH CITIZEN: Caesar's better parts
Shall be crowned in Brutus.

FIRST CITIZEN: We'll bring him to his house with shouts and clamours.

BRUTUS: My countrymen—

SECOND CITIZEN: Peace, silence, Brutus speaks.

FIRST CITIZEN: Peace ho!

Antony knows he is in trouble so he must go carefully. But as he proceeds his confidence rises. This change in his attitude demands close attention to:

- The tone of the speech.

   A line as simple as "Friends, Romans, countrymen, lend me your ears" has opportunities for experimenting. He might wait until the crowd quietens and then deliver the line in a normal tone of voice.

   He shouts over the noise of the mob, focusing their attention to him.

   He shouts the first three words, pauses and then quietly says "lend me your ears".

   Choose other lines in the speech that have different possibilities.

- The stressing of certain words.

   "... lend me your *ears*" or

   "... lend *me* your ears"

   What important difference does such a small change make? Antony repeats the words "Brutus is an honourable man" several times. How should these repetitions be handled to achieve the best effect?

BRUTUS: Good countrymen, let me depart alone,
And, for my sake, stay here with Antony.
Do grace to Caesar's corpse, and grace his speech
Tending to Caesar's glories, which Mark Antony,
By our permission, is allowed to make.
I do entreat you, not a man depart,   50
Save I alone, till Antony have spoke.

[Exit]

FIRST CITIZEN: Stay ho, and let us hear Mark Antony.
THIRD CITIZEN: Let him go up into the public chair.
We'll hear him. Noble Antony go up.
ANTONY: For Brutus' sake, I am beholding to you.

[Goes into the pulpit]

FOURTH CITIZEN: What does he say of Brutus?
THIRD CITIZEN: He says, for Brutus' sake
He finds himself beholding to us all.
FOURTH CITIZEN: 'Twere best he speak no harm of Brutus
here.   60
FIRST CITIZEN: This Caesar was a tyrant.
THIRD CITIZEN: Nay that's certain.
We are blest that Rome is rid of him.
SECOND CITIZEN: Peace, let us hear what Antony can say.
ANTONY: You gentle Romans—
CITIZENS: Peace ho, let us hear him.
ANTONY: Friends, Romans, countrymen, lend me your ears:
I come to bury Caesar, not to praise him.
The evil that men do lives after them,
The good is oft interred with their bones;   70
So let it be with Caesar. The noble Brutus
Hath told you Caesar was ambitious;
If it were so, it was a grievous fault,
And grievously hath Caesar answered it.
Here, under leave of Brutus and the rest—
For Brutus is an honourable man,
So are they all, all honourable men—
Come I to speak in Caesar's funeral.
He was my friend, faithful and just to me;
But Brutus says he was ambitious,   80
And Brutus is an honourable man.
He hath brought many captives home to Rome,
Whose ransoms did the general coffers fill.
Did this in Caesar seem ambitious?
When that the poor have cried, Caesar hath wept;
Ambition should be made of sterner stuff;
Yet Brutus says he was ambitious,
And Brutus is an honourable man.
You all did see that on the Lupercal

49

Towards the end of the first speech, Antony must know from the crowd's reaction that he is reaching them. How can he tell? As yet they have not said anything.

In the lines beginning "O judgement..." (Line 98) he becomes very emotional. Practise reading the lines concentrating on:
- any change of tone that is necessary.
- any pauses that add to the pathos.
- any action that shows his grief.

Do you agree with this critic on Antony's first speech?

Mark Antony speaks the first thirty-five lines of his address with delicacy, feeling his way, uncertain of his hearers. His pause ("I must pause till it come back to me") is a test of the strength of his position, fortified by a show of emotion ... it holds the crowd of citizens in suspense ... Antony may now proceed with a confidence he has earned and shrewdly pull out the rest of the stops.

J. L. Styan, Shakespeare's Stagecraft

Is the critic suggesting Antony is insincere?
Will your answer influence your reading?

I thrice presented him a kingly crown,   90
Which he did thrice refuse. Was this ambition?
Yet Brutus says he was ambitious,
And sure he is an honourable man.
I speak not to disprove what Brutus spoke,
But here I am to speak what I do know.
You all did love him once, not without cause;
What cause withholds you then to mourn for him?
O judgement, thou art fled to brutish beasts,
And men have lost their reason. Bear with me;
My heart is in the coffin there with Caesar,   100
And I must pause till it come back to me.
FIRST CITIZEN: Methinks there is much reason in his sayings.
SECOND CITIZEN: If thou consider rightly of the matter,
Caesar has had great wrong.
THIRD CITIZEN: Has he masters?
I fear there will a worse come in his place.
FOURTH CITIZEN: Marked ye his words? He would not take
the crown;
Therefore 'tis certain he was not ambitious.
FIRST CITIZEN: If it be found so, some will dear abide it.   110
SECOND CITIZEN: Poor soul, his eyes are red as fire with weeping.
THIRD CITIZEN: There's not a nobler man in Rome than Antony.
FOURTH CITIZEN: Now mark him, he begins again to speak.
ANTONY: But yesterday the word of Caesar might
Have stood against the world; now lies he there,
And none so poor to do him reverence.
O masters, if I were disposed to stir
Your hearts and minds to mutiny and rage,
I should do Brutus wrong, and Cassius wrong,   120
Who you all know are honourable men.
I will not do them wrong; I rather choose
To wrong the dead, to wrong myself and you,
Than I will wrong such honourable men.
But here's a parchment with the seal of Caesar;
I found it in his closet; 'tis his will.
Let but the commons hear this testament—
Which, pardon me, I do not mean to read—
And they would go and kiss dead Caesar's wounds,
And dip their napkins in his sacred blood,   130
Yea, beg a hair of him for memory,
And dying, mention it within their wills,
Bequeathing it as a rich legacy
Unto their issue.

The full excitement of the speeches cannot be achieved without disciplined work from the citizens. The mob needs to look chaotic and angry, without the scene becoming a mess.

Here is one way to achieve this discipline using all students in the classroom:

Choose four group leaders who will read the lines of the citizens. They must learn when to react and whether their reaction at a particular point is hostile, neutral or supportive.

Each group leader rehearses his group in an effort to produce an active, appropriate participation in the scene by every student. The crowd leader uses all the lines from the play and ad libs where it seems right at the time. These lines may be shouted out to Antony and Brutus, or the crowd in general, or may be addressed to a particular person in the crowd. The members of the group may echo the leader's comments or shout their own approval, suiting their actions to their words.

Each leader rehearses with his group while Brutus and Antony are preparing their speeches. (They should have fellow students helping them.)

Bring the crowd and the speakers together for a first trial and tape record the run through. The following questions may help:

- Is the crowd drowning out Antony? Are there times when such a drowning out is useful?
- Is the crowd too hesitant, inhibited or artificial?
- Can you bring in more variation? Are there times when they could speak differently—riotously, softly, threateningly?

After two or three attempts it might be useful to listen to a recording of professional actors performing the scene.

Look at Line 166. In the speech beginning "If you have tears..." there are several essential actions needed. For example: "You all do know this mantle..." Antony must pick up and show the cloak. What other examples can you find?

There are a lot of other possibilities for interpretative actions in Antony's speech. For example, in the line "Bear with me..." (Line 99), Antony could move down to the body and kneel while the crowd mutters. What other actions could add to the drama?

FOURTH CITIZEN: We'll hear the will. Read it Mark Antony.

ALL: The will, the will! We will hear Caesar's will.

ANTONY: Have patience gentle friends, I must not read it.
It is not meet you know how Caesar loved you.
You are not wood, you are not stones, but men;
And being men, hearing the will of Caesar,   140
It will inflame you, it will make you mad.
'Tis good you know not that you are his heirs;
For if you should, O what would come of it!

FOURTH CITIZEN: Read the will. We'll hear it Antony.
You shall read us the will, Caesar's will.

ANTONY: Will you be patient? Will you stay awhile?
I have o'ershot myself to tell you of it.
I fear I wrong the honourable men
Whose daggers have stabbed Caesar; I do fear it.

FOURTH CITIZEN: They were traitors. Honourable men!   150

ALL: The will! The testament!

SECOND CITIZEN: They were villains, murderers. The will,
read the will.

ANTONY: You will compel me then to read the will?
Then make a ring about the corpse of Caesar,
And let me show you him that made the will.
Shall I descend? And will you give me leave?

ALL: Come down.

SECOND CITIZEN: Descend.

THIRD CITIZEN: You shall have leave.   160

[Antony comes down]

FOURTH CITIZEN: A ring, stand round.

FIRST CITIZEN: Stand from the hearse, stand from the body.

SECOND CITIZEN: Room for Antony, most noble Antony.

ANTONY: Nay, press not so upon me; stand far off.

SEVERAL CITIZENS: Stand back; room; bear back.

ANTONY: If you have tears, prepare to shed them now.
You all do know this mantle. I remember
The first time ever Caesar put it on;
'Twas on a summer's evening in his tent,
That day he overcame the Nervii.   170
Look, in this place ran Cassius' dagger through.
See what a rent the envious Casca made.
Through this the well-beloved Brutus stabbed;
And as he plucked his cursed steel away,
Mark how the blood of Caesar followed it,
As rushing out of doors, to be resolved.
If Brutus so unkindly knocked or no;
For Brutus, as you know, was Caesar's angel.
Judge, O you gods, how dearly Caesar loved him.
This was the most unkindest cut of all;   180

Practise two readings of the closing lines of Antony's speech (Lines 231–250):
- emphasising his anguish, with his voice rising to a crescendo.
- using a quieter, more calculating tone.

Here is how one critic saw a performance of the scene:

Below the rostrum the mob shuffled and growled in the half-dark, an imprisoned animal impatient for release. Throughout Antony's speech, delivered with every wile of the political spellbinder, the superbly orchestrated whispers, murmurs, shouts, chants and screams deftly accompanied the shifting moods and rhythms of the harangue; and the continuous shuffle and stamp of their feet on the hollow, unpadded platform bear out a terrifying sound to their growing fury. Released at last at the peak of hysteria, they roared off the stage like a cyclone, mindless and deadly.

J. Ripley, *Julius Caesar on Stage in England and America 1599–1973*

For when the noble Caesar saw him stab,
Ingratitude, more strong than traitors' arms,
Quite vanquished him. Then burst his mighty heart;
And in his mantle muffling up his face,
Even at the base of Pompey's statue,
Which all the while ran blood, great Caesar fell.
O what a fall was there, my countrymen!
Then I, and you, and all of us fell down,
Whilst bloody treason flourished over us.
O now you weep, and I perceive you feel   190
The dint of pity. These are gracious drops.
Kind souls, what weep you when you but behold
Our Caesar's vesture wounded? Look you here,
Here is himself, marred as you see with traitors.

FIRST CITIZEN: O piteous spectacle!
SECOND CITIZEN: O noble Caesar!
THIRD CITIZEN: O woeful day!
FOURTH CITIZEN: O traitors, villains!
FIRST CITIZEN: O most bloody sight!
SECOND CITIZEN: We will be revenged.   200
ALL: Revenge! About! Seek! Burn! Fire! Kill! Slay!
      Let not a traitor live!
ANTONY: Stay countrymen.
FIRST CITIZEN: Peace there, hear the noble Antony.
SECOND CITIZEN: We'll hear him, we'll follow him, we'll die
      with him.
ANTONY: Good friends, sweet friends, let me not stir you up
      To such a sudden flood of mutiny.
      They that have done this deed are honourable.
      What private griefs they have, alas, I know not,   210
      That made them do it. They are wise and honourable,
      And will no doubt with reasons answer you.
      I come not friends, to steal away your hearts;
      I am no orator as Brutus is;
      But as you know me all, a plain blunt man,
      That love my friend; and that they know full well
      That gave me public leave to speak of him.
      For I have neither wit, nor words, nor worth,
      Action, nor utterance, nor the power of speech,
      To stir men's blood; I only speak right on.   220
      I tell you that which you yourselves do know,
      Show you sweet Caesar's wounds, poor poor dumb mouths,
      And I bid them speak for me. But were I Brutus,
      And Brutus Antony, there were an Antony
      Would ruffle up your spirits, and put a tongue
      In every wound of Caesar that should move
      The stones of Rome to rise and mutiny.
ALL: We'll mutiny.

The aim is to build up a scene of horror and tension. Merely for the citizens to rush in and kill Cinna would not achieve this dramatic tension. The following questions may help in building up the scene:

- Should Cinna come on before the arrival of the citizens or should they be there waiting?
- How do the citizens come on? All together? One at a time? Like shadows, waiting? What do they do as they wait?
- One group of students in working on the scene opened it with the citizens taunting Cinna with various indignities. For example, one pulled his nose. What else could they do?
- How does one time those actions to fit with the words?
- Does the pace change during the scene? For example, Cinna says "wisely I say, I am a bachelor". It is a joke. Does he not realise he is in danger? If so, at what point does he realise it and how do the tone and pace change?

FIRST CITIZEN: We'll burn the house of Brutus.

THIRD CITIZEN: Away then, come, seek the conspirators.   230

ANTONY: Yet hear me countrymen, yet hear me speak.

ALL: Peace ho, hear Antony, most noble Antony.

ANTONY: Why friends, you go to do you know not what.
    Wherein hath Caesar thus deserved your loves?
    Alas you know not. I must tell you then.
    You have forgot the will I told you of.

ALL: Most true. The will, let's stay and hear the will.

ANTONY: Here is the will, and under Caesar's seal.
    To every Roman citizen he gives,
    To every several man, seventy-five drachmas.   240

SECOND CITIZEN: Most noble Caesar! We'll revenge his death.

THIRD CITIZEN: O royal Caesar!

ANTONY: Hear me with patience.

ALL: Peace ho!

ANTONY: Moreover, he hath left you all his walks,
    His private arbours and new-planted orchards,
    On this side Tiber; he hath left them you,
    And to your heirs for ever—common pleasures,
    To walk abroad, and recreate yourselves.
    Here was a Caesar! When comes such another?   250

FIRST CITIZEN: Never, never. Come, away, away!
    We'll burn his body in the holy place,
    And with the brands fire the traitors' houses.
    Take up the body.

SECOND CITIZEN: Go fetch fire.

THIRD CITIZEN: Pluck down benches.

FOURTH CITIZEN: Pluck down forms, windows, any thing.

        [*Exeunt Citizens with the body*]

ANTONY: Now let it work. Mischief, thou art afoot,
    Take thou what course thou wilt.

Julius Caesar 3 (Act III, Scene III)
After the crowd has been aroused by Antony, it goes rioting and looting
through Rome. In this scene an innocent poet called Cinna is out walking.
He comes across some of the citizens in a street, and is taken for the
conspirator of the same name.

CINNA: I dreamt tonight that I did feast with Caesar,
    And things unluckily charge my fantasy.
    I have no will to wander forth of doors,
    Yet something leads me forth.

FIRST CITIZEN: What is your name?

SECOND CITIZEN: Whither are you going?

THIRD CITIZEN: Where do you dwell?

FOURTH CITIZEN: Are you a married man or a bachelor?

SECOND CITIZEN: Answer every man directly.

FIRST CITIZEN: Ay, and briefly.   10

FOURTH CITIZEN: Ay, and wisely.

THIRD CITIZEN: Ay, and truly, you were best.

CINNA: What is my name? Whither am I going? Where do I
dwell? Am I a married man or a bachelor? Then to answer
every man directly and briefly, wisely and truly—wisely I say,
I am a bachelor.

SECOND CITIZEN: That's as much as to say, they are fools that
marry. You'll bear me a bang for that I fear. Proceed directly.

CINNA: Directly I am going to Caesar's funeral.

FIRST CITIZEN: As a friend or an enemy?   20

CINNA: As a friend.

SECOND CITIZEN: That matter is answered directly.

FOURTH CITIZEN: For your dwelling—briefly.

CINNA: Briefly, I dwell by the Capitol.

THIRD CITIZEN: Your name sir, truly.

CINNA: Truly, my name is Cinna.

FIRST CITIZEN: Tear him to pieces, he's a conspirator.

CINNA: I am Cinna the poet, I am Cinna the poet.

FOURTH CITIZEN: Tear him for his bad verses, tear him for his
bad verses.   30

CINNA: I am not Cinna the conspirator.

FOURTH CITIZEN: It is no matter, his name's Cinna; pluck but
his name out of his heart, and turn him going.

THIRD CITIZEN: Tear him, tear him! Come, brands, ho! Fire
brands. To Brutus', to Cassius'; burn all. Some to Decius'
house, and some to Casca's; some to Ligarius'. Away, go!

[*Exeunt*]

GHOSTS

The task in this scene is to show there is "something terrible hanging over them".

How does the scene open? Will Francisco be on stage alone for some time? What would he be doing? Any sound effects? There are possibilities here for setting the atmosphere. John Gielgud said this of the opening:

The play should begin like a pistol shot. We don't want the usual striking bells and wind to give atmosphere. Francisco believes he has seen the Ghost and shouts out "Who's there?" suddenly and with great force.

Do you agree?

Study Line 10. Is there something behind Bernardo's question "Have you had quiet guard?"

What is the tone of Horatio's line "Tush, tush, 'twill not appear"? (Line 37)

Hamlet (Act I, Scene I)

This is the first scene of *Hamlet*. The guards on a previous night claim to have seen the ghost of the King who has recently died. They ask Horatio to join them to watch for the ghost.

[A platform before the castle. Francisco at his post. Enter to him Bernardo]

BERNARDO: Who's there?

FRANCISCO: Nay, answer me: stand and unfold yourself.

BERNARDO: Long live the king!

FRANCISCO: Bernardo?

BERNARDO: He.

FRANCISCO: You come most carefully upon your hour.

BERNARDO: 'Tis now struck twelve; get thee to bed, Francisco.

FRANCISCO: For this relief much thanks: 'tis bitter cold,
    And I am sick at heart.

BERNARDO: Have you had quiet guard?   10

FRANCISCO: Not a mouse stirring.

BERNARDO: Well, good night.
    If you do meet Horatio and Marcellus,
    The rivals of my watch, bid them make haste.

FRANCISCO: I think I hear them. Stand, ho! Who is there?

[Enter Horatio and Marcellus]

HORATIO: Friends to this ground.

MARCELLUS: And liegemen to the Dane.

FRANCISCO: Give you good night.

MARCELLUS: O, farewell, honest soldier:
    Who hath relieved you?   20

FRANCISCO: Bernardo has my place.
    Give you good night.

[Exit]

MARCELLUS: Holla! Bernardo!

BERNARDO: Say,—
    What, is Horatio there?

HORATIO: A piece of him.

BERNARDO: Welcome, Horatio: welcome, good Marcellus.

MARCELLUS: What, has this thing appear'd again to-night?

BERNARDO: I have seen nothing.

MARCELLUS: Horatio says 'tis but our fantasy,   30
    And will not let belief take hold of him
    Touching this dreaded sight, twice seen of us:
    Therefore I have entreated him along
    With us to watch the minutes of this night;
    That, if again this apparition come,
    He may approve our eyes and speak to it.

HORATIO: Tush, tush, 'twill not appear.

Practise various ways of reading Bernardo's speech, Lines 44–48. A common way is for his voice to rise in tension and anxiety until it is broken off with the unfinished sentence. Are the "B's" in the line "The bell then beating one" important?

Practise reading Lines 50–62. The terror must be achieved by voice alone. A successful reading' will take into account volume, pitch and pace. For example, would you agree that the tone changes with Horatio's speech beginning "What art thou that ...?"

A famous Shakespearean producer, John Gielgud, said this about this scene:

The words of these opening lines must have height to give the sense of the open air. As it must be dark, the words must be pitched very clearly or they will not be heard. (Gielgud repeats the opening lines four times.) Don't set your readings. You've got to listen and refresh your ear each time. Keep the feeling of the cold. You've got to walk about to keep your circulation going. They all know there is something in the woodshed, yet they won't speak of it openly. There is so much they *don't* say in this scene. That's what's interesting—what is understood. People still go about their business, doing what they have to do, but with a terrible shadow hanging over them—like in the war. One does it with a heavy heart and this must be conveyed.

R. Sterne, *John Gielgud Directs Richard Burton in Hamlet*

BERNARDO: Sit down awhile;
    And let us once again assail your ears,
    That are so fortified against our story,   40
    What we two nights have seen.
HORATIO: Well, sit we down,
    And let us hear Bernardo speak of this.
BERNARDO: Last night of all,
    When yond same star that's westward from the pole
    Had made his course to illume that part of heaven
    Where now it burns, Marcellus and myself,
    The bell then beating one,—
MARCELLUS: Peace, break thee off; look, where it comes again!

[Enter Ghost]

BERNARDO: In the same figure, like the king that's dead.   50
MARCELLUS: Thou art a scholar; speak to it, Horatio.
BARNARDO: Looks it not like the king? Mark it, Horatio.
HORATIO: Most like: it harrows me with fear and wonder.
BERNARDO: It would be spoke to.
MARCELLUS: Question it, Horatio.
HORATIO: What art thou that usurp'st this time of night,
    Together with that fair and warlike form
    In which the majesty of buried Denmark
    Did sometimes march? By heaven I charge thee, speak!
MARCELLUS: It is offended.   60
BERNARDO: See, it stalks away!
HORATIO: Stay! speak, speak! I charge thee, speak!

[Exit Ghost.]

The main question to work on in this scene is: what is the general mood of the scene and how can one achieve that mood?

Note how Brutus treats his soldiers and servant. Can their behaviour contribute to the mood of the scene?

There will be periods of silence, some quite lengthy. Mark in where these silences occur.

What sound effects can contribute to the mood? Of course Lucius must play the instrument. But are there times when other sound effects could help?

Is there a change of mood at the entry of the ghost? If so, how can it be achieved? For example, is there any change in speed, pitch or tone as Brutus sees the ghost? What does Brutus do as he sees the ghost and after it disappears?

Divide your page into two columns. In the left hand column make a list of the props that are necessary. In the right hand column write down how these props will be used and on what lines.

Props	Actions
Book	Brutus begins reading ...

Julius Caesar (Act IV, Scene III)

Brutus and Cassius flee after Antony has turned the crowd against them. Things are turning very much against Brutus. He has just had a violent argument with Cassius, one of the conspirators, and has recently received news of his wife's death. These scenes of violence and extreme emotions are followed by this scene of a very different mood. Brutus is in his tent; he is saying good night to his soldiers, Varro and Claudius, and asks his servant Lucius to play him some music.

[Enter Varro and Claudius]

VARRO: Calls my lord?

BRUTUS: I pray you, sirs, lie in my tent and sleep;
It may be I shall raise you by and by
On business to my brother Cassius.

VARRO: So please you we will stand and watch your pleasure.

BRUTUS: I will not have it so. Lie down, good sirs;
It may be I shall otherwise bethink me.
Look, Lucius, here's the book I sought for so;
I put it in the pocket of my gown.

[Varro and Claudius lie down]

LUCIUS: I was sure your lordship did not give it me.   10

BRUTUS: Bear with me, good boy, I am much forgetful.
Canst thou hold up thy heavy eyes awhile,
And touch thy instrument a strain or two?

LUCIUS: Ay, my lord, an't please you.

BRUTUS: It does, my boy.
I trouble thee too much, but thou art willing.

LUCIUS: It is my duty, sir.

BRUTUS: I should not urge thy duty past thy might;
I know young bloods look for a time of rest.

LUCIUS: I have slept, my lord, already.   20

BRUTUS: It was well done; and thou shalt sleep again;
I will not hold thee long. If I do live,
I will be good to thee.

[Music and a song. Lucius falls asleep]

This is a sleepy tune. O murd'rous slumber!
Layest thou thy leaden mace upon my boy,
That plays thee music? Gentle knave, good night.
I will not do thee so much wrong to wake thee.
If thou dost nod, thou break'st thy instrument;
I'll take it from thee: and, good boy, good night.
Let me see, let me see; is not the leaf turn'd down   30
Where I left reading? Here it is, I think.

[Sits down. Enter the Ghost of Caesar]

How ill this taper burns! Ha! who comes here?
I think it is the weakness of mine eyes

Divide another page into two columns. What other props might be useful in the scene but are not mentioned in the text? In the right hand column note any interpretative actions using these props.

Props	Actions
A cloak for Brutus	As Lucius falls asleep Brutus takes off his cloak and puts it around Lucius to keep him warm.

That shapes this monstrous apparition.
It comes upon me. Art thou any thing?
Art thou some god, some angel, or some devil,
That mak'st my blood cold and my hair to stare?
Speak to me what thou art.

GHOST: Thy evil spirit, Brutus.

BRUTUS: Why com'st thou?   40

GHOST: To tell thee thou shalt see me at Philippi.

BRUTUS: Well; then I shall see thee again?

GHOST: Ay, at Philippi.

BRUTUS: Why, I will see thee at Philippi, then.

[Exit Ghost.]

Now I have taken heart thou vanishest.
Ill spirit, I would hold more talk with thee.
Boy! Lucius! Varro! Claudius! Sirs, awake!
Claudius!

LUCIUS: The strings, my lord, are false.

BRUTUS: He thinks he still is at his instrument.   50
Lucius, awake!

LUCIUS: My lord!

BRUTUS: Didst thou dream, Lucius, that thou so criedst out?

LUCIUS: My lord, I do not know that I did cry.

BRUTUS: Yes, that thou didst. Didst thou see any thing?

LUCIUS: Nothing, my lord.

BRUTUS: Sleep again, Lucius. Sirrah Claudius!
[To Varro] Fellow thou, awake!

VARRO: My lord?

CLAUDIUS: My lord?   60

BRUTUS: Why did you so cry out, sirs, in your sleep?

BOTH: Did we, my lord?

BRUTUS: Ay. Saw you any thing?

VARRO: No, my lord, I saw nothing.

CLAUDIUS: Nor I, my lord.

BRUTUS: Go and commend me to my brother Cassius;
Bid him set on his pow'rs betimes before,
And we will follow.

VARRO AND CLAUDIUS: It shall be done, my lord.

[Exeunt]

MOMENTS OF TENSION

What are the main fears of Juliet?

Examine the first ten lines. What different emotions does Juliet experience? Mark in where the tone changes.

Divide the scene into sections, each section showing a different emotion. For example, the scene probably begins quietly and finishes close to frenzy. Her fears, doubts, and assurances require changes of speed and rhythm together with pauses in speaking. Practise these changes in reading.

The following drama critic shows how the length of syllables can influence a reading:

The thought of waiting in the tomb at first hurries her tongue, until she catches her breath at the prospect, with a pause in "There's a fearful point". As her imagination works the breathlessly long syllables of "To whose foul mouth no healthsome air breathes in" recreates the horror in her mind.

J. L. Styan, *Shakespearean Stagecraft*

Do you agree with this view?

Make two columns on the page. On the left make a list of the essential props and on the right state how they are used.

Props	Use
A dagger	She picks it up

Make another two columns. On the left make a list of props that are not essential but may be useful, and on the right state how they are used.

Props	Use
A wedding dress	She takes it and quietly puts it away

Romeo and Juliet 1 (Act IV, Scene III)
Read the earlier sections of the play. Romeo and Juliet are in love and have married secretly. Juliet's father insists that she marry the man of his choice, Paris. The Friar prepares a plan: on the night before the wedding she is to take a potion that will put her to sleep; her parents will think her dead. She will be taken to the family tomb. When she wakes Romeo will be there and they will flee together. In this scene Juliet is in her room alone. She has just said good night to the nurse and prepares to take the potion.

JULIET: Farewell. God knows when we shall meet again.
    I have a faint cold fear thrills through my veins,
    That almost freezes up the heat of life.
    I'll call them back again to comfort me.
    Nurse! What should she do here?
    My dismal scene I needs must act alone.
    Come vial.
    What if this mixture do not work at all?
    Shall I be married then tomorrow morning?
    No, no, this shall forbid it. Lie thou there.   10

[Lays down a dagger]

    What if it be a poison which the friar
    Subtly hath ministered to have me dead,
    Lest in this marriage he should be dishonoured,
    Because he married me before to Romeo?
    I fear it is, and yet methinks it should not,
    For he hath still been tried a holy man.
    How if when I am laid into the tomb,
    I wake before the time that Romeo
    Come to redeem me? There's a fearful point.
    Shall I not then be stifled in the vault,   20
    To whose foul mouth no healthsome air breathes in,
    And there die strangled ere my Romeo comes?
    Or if I live, is it not very like,
    The horrible conceit of death and night,
    Together with the terror of the place—
    As in a vault, an ancient receptacle,
    Where for this many hundred years the bones
    Of all my buried ancestors are packed,
    Where bloody Tybalt yet but green in earth
    Lies festering in his shroud, where as they say,   30
    At some hours in the night spirits resort—
    Alack, alack, is it not like that I,
    So early waking—what with loathsome smells,
    And shrieks like mandrakes' torn out of the earth,
    That living mortals hearing them, run mad—
    O if I wake, shall I not be distraught,
    Environed with all these hideous fears,

Practise reading Lines 42–45 in the following ways:
- She screams them in terror.
- She is so frightened she can scarcely move or speak and speaks them almost in a whisper.

ROMEO: Tush, thou art deceived,

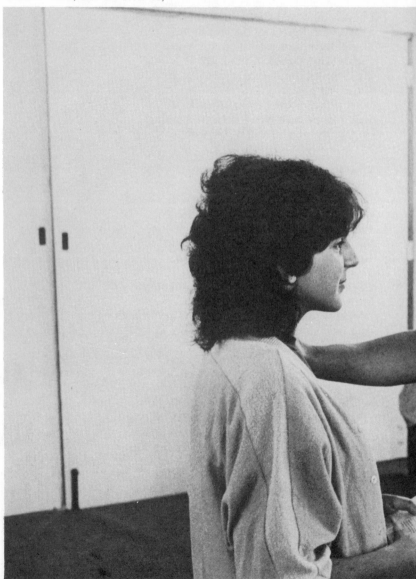

And madly play with my forefathers' joints,
And pluck the mangled Tybalt from his shroud,
And in this rage, with some great kinsman's bone, 40
As with a club, dash out my desperate brains?
O look, methinks I see my cousin's ghost
Seeking out Romeo that did spit his body
Upon a rapier's point—stay Tybalt, stay!
Romeo! Romeo! Romeo! I drink to thee.

[She falls upon her bed within the curtains]

Before reading this scene make up your own dialogue and actions for the scene. Balthasar arrives to tell the news. What happens? How would he present the news? How would Romeo react? What would he say?

What was the general mood of the scenes you made up? Many students in acting the scene seem to think it should be read with Romeo shouting and raving. Here are two critics on the scene:

Leigh (the actor) also made a mistake in allowing Romeo to *faint ridiculously* in his servant's arms when he hears of Juliet's death, and then to recover sufficiently to bellow "I defy you, stars", as if he expected his voice to reach them. These words should be spoken in a low intense voice.

G. Gosse, *Shakespeare's Plays 1890–1952*

Romeo's hearing of Juliet's death is best taken with a terrible quiet and a mad glint in the eye giving a new depth to contrast with his earlier abandon.

G. Wilson Knight, *Principles of Shakespearean Production*

In the light of these comments would you make any changes to your improvised scenes?

Divide your page into two columns. On the left write the sentence from the text. On the right write what you think is happening.

Text	Interpretation
"News from Verona."	Joyful news; he greets Balthasar warmly.
"That I ask again,"	He falters because he senses something is wrong.

Romeo and Juliet 2 (Act V, Scene I)

Balthasar, Romeo's servant, hears of the "death" of Juliet. He does not know of the plan. He rushes to Romeo, who is waiting outside the city, to tell him of the terrible news.

[Enter Balthasar]

ROMEO: News from Verona. How now Balthasar,
    Dost thou not bring me letters from the friar?
    How doth my lady? Is my father well?
    How doth my Juliet? That I ask again,
    For nothing can be ill if she be well.

BALTHASAR: Then she is well and nothing can be ill.
    Her body sleeps in Capels' monument,
    And her immortal part with angels lives.
    I saw her laid low in her kindred's vault,
    And presently took post to tell it you.   10
    O pardon me for bringing these ill news,
    Since you did leave it for my office sir.

ROMEO: Is it even so? Then I defy you, stars.
    Thou knowest my lodging, get me ink and paper
    And hire post-horses; I will hence tonight.

BALTHASAR: I do beseech you sir, have patience.
    Your looks are pale and wild, and do import
    Some misadventure.

ROMEO: Tush, thou art deceived,
    Leave me, and do the thing I bid thee do.   20
    Hast thou no letters to me from the friar?

BALTHASAR: No my good lord.

ROMEO: No matter. Get thee gone,

[Exit Balthasar]

Before reading this scene make up your own dialogue. Romeo finds Juliet dead. He kills himself with poison. Juliet awakes and kills herself with a dagger.

In your work be mindful of:
- The passion but the tenderness.
- Romeo's strength and self-control.
- Juliet's anguish.

Make a list of the number of essential movements that are in Romeo's speech. For example, after addressing Juliet, he sees the body of Tybalt. He will then move across to the body.

Make a list of the movements that could add to the drama of the scene. For example, as Romeo says "Forgive me cousin", he kneels at Tybalt's tomb and prays quietly.

The following questions could help in the reading of Romeo's speech:
- Where should Juliet's body be placed?
- How does Romeo die?
- Does he give way to tears?
- Does he bring a candle on with him?
- In what way can he take his last embrace?

Look at Juliet's speech, "O comfortable friar..." How is it said: in a sleepy way, with unease, with growing fear?

Romeo hastens to Juliet's tomb. He finds Juliet "dead". He poisons himself
with a substance he has purchased from an apothecary. Juliet wakes to find
his dead body. The Friar arrives and tries to persuade her to flee; she refuses.

ROMEO:　How oft when men are at the point of death
　　　　Have they been merry, which their keepers call
　　　　A lightning before death. O how may I
　　　　Call this a lightning? O my love, my wife!—
　　　　Death that hath sucked the honey of thy breath,
　　　　Hath had no power yet upon thy beauty.
　　　　Thou art not conquered; beauty's ensign yet
　　　　Is crimson in thy lips and in thy cheeks,
　　　　And death's pale flag is not advanced there.　　　　10
　　　　Tybalt, liest thou there in thy bloody sheet?
　　　　O what more favour can I do to thee,
　　　　Than with that hand that cut thy youth in twain
　　　　To sunder his that was thine enemy?
　　　　Forgive me cousin. Ah dear Juliet,
　　　　Why art thou yet so fair? Shall I believe
　　　　That unsubstantial death is amorous,
　　　　And that the lean abhorred monster keeps
　　　　Thee here in dark to be his paramour?
　　　　For fear of that, I still will stay with thee,　　　　20
　　　　And never from this palace of dim night
　　　　Depart again. Here, here will I remain
　　　　With worms that are thy chamber-maids. O here
　　　　Will I set up my everlasting rest;
　　　　And shake the yoke of inauspicious stars
　　　　From this world-wearied flesh. Eyes look your last.
　　　　Arms, take your last embrace. And lips, O you
　　　　The doors of breath, seal with a righteous kiss
　　　　A dateless bargain to engrossing death.　　　　30
　　　　[Takes out the poison]　Come bitter conduct, come unsavoury guide,
　　　　Thou desperate pilot, now at once run on
　　　　The dashing rocks thy sea-sick weary bark.
　　　　Here's to my love *[Drinks]*　O true apothecary!
　　　　Thy drugs are quick. Thus with a kiss I die.
　　　　　　　　　　[Friar enters]
FRIAR:　Romeo!
　　　　And steeped in blood? Ah what an unkind hour
　　　　Is guilty of this lamentable chance!
　　　　The lady stirs.

　　　　　　　　　　[Juliet rises]

JULIET:　O comfortable friar, where is my lord?　　　　40
　　　　I do remember well where I should be,
　　　　And there I am. Where is my Romeo?

Draw a stage plan of the scene making sure that all props and characters mentioned in the text are included.

FRIAR LAWRENCE: I hear some noise. Lady, come from that nest
    Of death, contagion, and unnatural sleep.
    A greater power than we can contradict
    Hath thwarted our intents. Come, come away.
    Thy husband in thy bosom there lies dead;
    And Paris too. Come I'll dispose of thee
    Among a sisterhood of holy nuns.
    Stay not to question, for the watch is coming.   50
    Come, go good Juliet, I dare no longer stay.

              [Exit Friar Lawrence]

JULIET: Go get thee hence, for I will not away.
    What's here? A cup closed in my true love's hand?
    Poison I see hath been his timeless end.
    O churl, drunk all, and left no friendly drop
    To help me after? I will kiss thy lips;
    Haply some poison yet doth hang on them,
    To make me die with a restorative.
    Thy lips are warm.
FIRST WATCH: *[Within]* Lead, boy. Which way?   60
JULIET: Yea, noise? Then I'll be brief. O happy dagger!

              [Draws Romeo's dagger]

    This is thy sheath; there rest, and let me die.
              [She stabs herself]

FUNNY SCENES

The following general points may help in making the play amusing:

Experiment with different accents and ages for the voices.

It may help to have girls playing the more boisterous parts (Pyramus and Lion) and boys playing the gentler parts (Thisby and Moonshine). Bottom is very conceited about his main role and he overacts dreadfully. What mannerisms can show his conceit and his showing off?

Flute is playing a sophisticated lady. The laughs must be achieved by showing that he has none of the qualities of a lady.

As the Prologue is spoken how can each character be introduced in his or her role? How can some of the absurd comments of the Prologue be emphasised?

Wall is very nervous about his part. How can his nervousness be shown? Also how can you show him to be very slow and heavy?

What can you make of Pyramus' "O's"?

If Thisby is played by a girl, she should emphasise a boy's mannerisms; if played by a boy, he should try to be as feminine as possible.

Lion is played by a very gentle person. His roaring must be as unconvincing as possible.

How does Moonshine react to Pyramus' dying?

A Midsummer Night's Dream (Act V, Scene I)

Theseus, Duke of Athens, has arranged for a group of amateur actors to perform a play on his wedding day. The play is supposed to be a tragedy but the actors are so bad and the lines so silly that the result must be as absurd and as funny as possible. The characters are: Nick Bottom as Pyramus, Peter Quince as Prologue, Snug as Lion, Francis Flute as Thisby, Robin Starveling as Moonshine, and Tom Snout as Wall.

PROLOGUE: If we offend, it is with our good will.
    That you should think, we come not to offend,
    But with good will. To show our simple skill,
    That is the true beginning of our end.
    Consider, then, we come but in despite.
    We do not come, as minding to content you,
    Our true intent is. All for your delight,
    We are not here. That you should here repent you,
    The actors are at hand; and, by their show,
    You shall know all, that you are like to know.   10

[Enter Pyramus and Thisby and Wall and Moonshine
and Lion (as in dumbshow)]

    Gentles, perchance you wonder at this show;
    But wonder on, till truth make all things plain.
    This man is Pyramus, if you would know;
    This beauteous lady Thisby is certain.
    This man, with lime and roughcast, doth present
    Wall, that vile Wall which did these lovers sunder;
    And through Wall's chink, poor souls, they are content
    To whisper. At the which let no man wonder.
    This man, with lantern, dog, and bush of thorn,
    Presenteth Moonshine; for, if you will know,   20
    By moonshine did these lovers think no scorn
    To meet at Ninus' tomb, there, there to woo.
    This grisly beast, which Lion hight by name,
    The trusty Thisby, coming first by night,
    Did scare away, or rather did affright;
    And, as she fled, her mantle she did fall,
    Which Lion vile with bloody mouth did stain.
    Anon comes Pyramus, sweet youth and tall,
    And finds his trusty Thisby's mantle slain:
    Whereat, with blade, with bloody blameful blade,   30
    He bravely broached his boiling bloody breast;
    And Thisby, tarrying in mulberry shade,
    His dagger drew, and died. For all the rest,
    Let Lion, Moonshine, Wall, and lovers twain
    At large discourse, while here they do remain.

[Exit Lion, Thisby and Moonshine]

How can Pyramus' "death" be made as funny as possible?
The following are suggestions:

- His sword sticks in his scabbard.
- His sword cuts his fingers.
- He takes a very long time to die.
- He is annoyed with Moonshine.

What other suggestions can you make?

How can you make Thisby's "death" amusing?

WALL: In this same interlude it doth befall
        That I, one Snout by name, present a wall;
        And such a wall, as I would have you think,
        That had in it a crannied hole or chink,
        Through which the lovers, Pyramus and Thisby,   40
        Did whisper often very secretly.
        This loam, this roughcast, and this stone, doth show
        That I am that same wall; the truth is so;
        And this the cranny is, right and sinister,
        Through which the fearful lovers are to whisper.

PYRAMUS: O grim-looked night! O night with hue so black!
        O night, which ever art when day is not!
        O night, O night! Alack, alack, alack,
        I fear my Thisby's promise is forgot!
        And thou, O wall, O sweet, O lovely wall,   50
        That stand'st between her father's ground and mine!
        Thou wall, O wall, O sweet and lovely wall,
        Show me thy chink, to blink through with mine eyne!

                    [Wall holds up his fingers]

        Thanks, courteous wall. Jove shield thee well for this!
        But what see I? No Thisby do I see.
        O wicked wall, through whom I see no bliss!
        Cursed be thy stones for thus deceiving me!

                    [Enter Thisby]

THISBY: O wall, full often hast thou heard my moans,
        For parting my fair Pyramus and me!
        My cherry lips have often kissed thy stones,   60
        Thy stones with lime and hair knit up in thee.
PYRAMUS: I see a voice: now will I to the chink,
        To spy an I can hear my Thisby's face.
        Thisby!
THISBY: My love thou art, my love I think.
PYRAMUS: Think what thou wilt, I am thy lover's grace;
        And, like Limander, am I trusty still.
THISBY: And I like Helen, till the Fates me kill.
PYRAMUS: Not Shafalus to Procrus was so true.
THISBY: As Shafalus to Procrus, I to you.   70
PYRAMUS: O kiss me through the hole of this vile wall!
THISBY: I kiss the wall's hole, not your lips at all.
PYRAMUS: Wilt thou at Ninny's tomb meet me straightway?
THISBY: Tide life, 'tide death, I come without delay.

                    [Exeunt Pyramus and Thisby]

[Enter Lion and Moonshine]

LION: You ladies, you, whose gentle hearts do fear
    The smallest monstrous mouse that creeps on floor,
    May now perchance both quake and tremble here,
    When lion rough in wildest rage doth roar.
    Then know that I, as Snug the joiner, am
    A lion fell, nor else no lion's dam;   80
    For, if I should as lion come in strife
    Into this place, 'twere pity on my life.
MOONSHINE: This lanthorn doth the hornèd moon present—
MOONSHINE: This lanthorn doth the hornèd moon present;
    Myself the man i' th' moon do seem to be.
MOONSHINE: All that I have to say is to tell you that
    the lanthorn is the moon; I, the man i' th' moon;
    this thorn bush, my thorn bush; and this dog, my dog.

[Enter Thisby]

THISBY: This is old Ninny's tomb. Where is my love?
LION: Oh—   90

[The lion roars. Thisby runs off.]

[Enter Pyramus]

PYRAMUS: Sweet Moon, I thank thee for thy sunny beams;
    I thank thee, Moon, for shining now so bright;
    For, by thy gracious, golden, glittering gleams,
        I trust to take of truest Thisby sight.
            But stay, O spite!
            But mark, poor knight,
    What dreadful dole is here!
            Eyes, do you see?
            How can it be?
    O dainty duck! O dear!   100
            Thy mantle good,
            What, stained with blood!
    Approach, ye Furies fell!
            O Fates, come, come,
            Cut thread and thrum;
    Quail, crush, conclude, and quell!

PYRAMUS: O wherefore, Nature, didst thou lions frame?
    Since lion vile hath here deflow'red my dear:
    Which is—no, no—which was the fairest dame
    That lived, that loved, that liked, that looked with cheer.   110
                Come, tears, confound;
                Out, sword, and wound
            The pap of Pyramus;
               Ay, that left pap,
               Where heart doth hop.

[Stabs himself]

Thus die I, thus, thus, thus.
  Now am I dead.
  Now am I fled;
My soul is in the sky.
  Tongue, lose thy light;   120
  Moon, take thy flight.

        [Exit Moonshine]
Now die, die, die, die, die.

        [Dies]

THISBY: Asleep, my love?
  What, dead, my dove?
O Pyramus, arise!
  Speak, speak. Quite dumb?
  Dead, dead? A tomb
Must cover thy sweet eyes.
  These lily lips,
  This cherry nose,   130
These yellow cowslip cheeks,
  Are gone, are gone.
  Lovers, make moan.
His eyes were green as leeks.
  O Sisters Three,
  Come, come to me,
With hands as pale as milk;
  Lay them in gore,
  Since you have shore
With shears his thread of silk.   140
  Tongue, not a word.
  Come, trusty sword,
Come, blade, my breast imbrue!

        [Stabs herself]

And, farewell, friends.
Thus Thisby ends.
Adieu, adieu, adieu.

        [Dies]

Mime Malvolio as a conceited person strutting around like a peacock.

Do the same mime again but put your own words to it.

Make a sketch plan of the stage showing where they are hiding, what props are necessary, and where Malvolio moves.

Bring out the comedy by concentrating on such exaggerated antics as: the business of hiding; Sir Toby's uncontrollable fury; the excitement of the preparation as they see him coming; the asides that cannot be heard by Malvolio; what he does during the asides; the fact that he does not see the other three but is perhaps at times suspicious; Malvolio's antics as he deludes himself, his smile, his little dances of joy, his daydreaming.

Sir Toby calls him an "overweening rogue". What other names can you find applied to Malvolio? In acting out the scene try to make the names seem justified.

Twelfth Night (Act II, Scene V)

Malvolio is the servant of a very rich lady, Olivia. Staying in Olivia's house are her uncle, Sir Toby Belch, who spends his time drinking, and a very foolish knight, Sir Andrew Aguecheek. Malvolio does not approve of either of these, nor of Maria, Olivia's maid. Malvolio reports them all to Olivia for drunkenness and they plan their revenge. Maria forges a love letter for Malvolio in Olivia's handwriting and drops it in the garden for Malvolio to find. Malvolio not only has a secret passion for Olivia but he is also ambitious and wants to rise on the social scale. Maria, Sir Toby, Sir Andrew and Fabian (another servant) watch from behind a hedge as Malvolio finds the letter.

MARIA: Get ye all three into the box tree. Malvolio's coming down this walk. He has been yonder i' the sun practising behaviour to his own shadow this half hour. Observe him, for the love of mockery; for I know this letter will make a contemplative idiot of him. Close, in the name of jesting. *[The others hide]* Lie thou there *[throws down a letter]*; for here comes the trout that must be caught with tickling.

[Exit. Enter Malvolio]

MALVOLIO: 'Tis but fortune; all is fortune. Maria once told me she did affect me; and I have heard herself come thus near, that should she fancy, it should be one of my complexion. Besides,   **10** she uses me with a more exalted respect than anyone else that follows her. What should I think on't?

TOBY: Here's an overweening rogue.

FABIAN: O, peace! Contemplation makes a rare turkey cock of him. How he jets under his advanced plumes!

ANDREW: Slight, I could so beat the rogue.

TOBY: Peace, I say.

MALVOLIO: To be Count Malvolio.

TOBY: Ah, rogue!

ANDREW: Pistol him, pistol him.   **20**

TOBY: Peace, peace.

MALVOLIO: There is example for't. The Lady of the Strachy married the yeoman of the wardrobe.

ANDREW: Fie on him, Jezebel.

FABIAN: O, peace! Now he's deeply in. Look how imagination blows him.

MALVOLIO: Having been three months married to her, sitting in my state—

TOBY: O for a stone-bow, to hit him in the eye!

MALVOLIO: Calling my officers about me, in my branched velvet   **30** gown; having come from a day-bed, where I have left Olivia sleeping—

TOBY: Fire and brimstone!

FABIAN: O, peace, peace!

Improvise the scene when he meets Olivia. One critic sees the scene like this:

> His physical performance says most; perhaps he trips over his own feet ... or he may tremble and stutter as if inwardly afraid; or he may work hard, smiling and ogling; or he could relapse into giggling. Then he delivers a prepared speech to Olivia, not hearing any of the interjections which attempt to stop him.
>
> J. Russell Brown, *Discovering Shakespeare*

MALVOLIO: And then to have the humour of state; and after a
  demure travel of regard, telling them I know my place, as I
  would they should do theirs, to ask for my kinsman Toby—
TOBY: Bolts and shackles!
FABIAN: O peace, peace, peace, now, now.
MALVOLIO: Seven of my people, with an obedient start, make out   40
  for him. I frown the while, and perchance wind up my watch,
  or play with my—some rich jewel. Toby approaches; curtsies
  there to me—
TOBY: Shall this fellow live?
FABIAN: Though our silence be drawn from us with cars, yet peace.
MALVOLIO: I extend my hand to him thus, quenching my familiar
  smile with an austere regard of control—
TOBY: And does not Toby take you a blow o' the lips then?
MALVOLIO: Saying, "Cousin Toby, my fortunes having
  cast me on your niece, give me this prerogative of speech."   50
TOBY: What, what?
MALVOLIO: "You must amend your drunkenness."
TOBY: Out, scab!
FABIAN: Nay, patience, or we break the sinews of our plot.
MALVOLIO: "Besides, you waste the treasure of your time
  with a foolish knight—"
ANDREW: That's me, I warrant you.
MALVOLIO: "One Sir Andrew—"
ANDREW: I knew 'twas I, for many do call me fool.
MALVOLIO: What employment have we here?   60

[Takes up the letter]

FABIAN: Now is the woodcock near the gin.
TOBY: O peace, and the spirit of humours intimate reading aloud
  to him!
MALVOLIO: By my life this is my lady's hand. These be her very
  C's, her U's, and her T's; and thus makes she her great P's. It
  is, in contempt of question, her hand.
ANDREW: Her C's, her U's, and her T's? Why that?
MALVOLIO: *[reads]* "To the unknown beloved, this, and my good
  wishes." Her very phrases! By your leave, wax. Soft, and the
  impressure her Lucrece, with which she uses to seal. 'Tis my   70
  lady. To whom should this be?
FABIAN: This wins him, liver and all.
MALVOLIO: *[reads]*
      "Jove Knows I love,
        But who?
      Lips, do not move;
        No man must know."
  "No man must know." What follows? The numbers
  altered! "No man must know." If this should be thee,
  Malvolio?

TOBY: Marry, hang thee, brock!

MALVOLIO: *[reads]*
  "I may command where I adore,
   But silence, like a Lucrece knife,
  With bloodless stroke my heart doth gore.
   M. O. A. I. doth sway my life."

FABIAN: A fustian riddle.

TOBY: Excellent wench, say I.

MALVOLIO: "M. O. A. I. doth sway my life." Nay, but
 first, let me see, let me see, let me see.

FABIAN: What dish o' poison has she dressed him!

TOBY: And with what wing the staniel checks at it!

MALVOLIO: "I may command where I adore." Why, she may
 command me: I serve her; she is my lady. Why, this is evident
 to any formal capacity. There is no obstruction in this. And
 the end; what should that alphabetical position portend? If I
 could make that resemble something in me! Softly, "M. O. A.
 I."

TOBY: O, ay, make up that. He is now at a cold scent.

FABIAN: Sowter will cry upon't for all this, though it be as rank as
 a fox.

MALVOLIO: M.—Malvolio. M.—Why, that begins my name.

FABIAN: Did not I say he would work it out? The cur is excellent
 at faults.

MALVOLIO: M.—But then there is no consonancy in the sequel.
 That suffers under probation. A should follow, but O does.

FABIAN: And O shall end, I hope.

TOBY: Ay, or I'll cudgel him, and make him cry O.

MALVOLIO: And then I comes behind.

FABIAN: Ay, an you had any eye behind you, you might see more
 detraction at your heels than fortunes before you.

MALVOLIO: M, O, A, I. This simulation is not as the former; and
 yet, to crush this a little, it would bow to me, for every one of
 these letters are in my name. Soft, here follows prose.
 [Reads] "If this fall into thy hand, revolve. In my stars I am
 above thee, but be not afraid of greatness. Some are born great,
 some achieve greatness, and some have greatness thrust upon
 'em. Thy Fates open their hands; let thy blood and spirit
 embrace them; and to inure thyself to what thou art like to be,
 cast thy humble slough and appear fresh. Be opposite with a
 kinsman, surly with servants. Let thy tongue tang arguments
 of state; put thyself into the trick of singularity. She thus advises
 thee that sighs for thee. Remember who commended thy yellow
 stockings and wished to see thee ever cross-gartered. I say,
 remember. Go to, thou art made, if thou desir'st to be so. If
 not, let me see thee a steward still, the fellow of servants, and
 not worthy to touch Fortune's fingers. Farewell. She that would
 alter services with thee,

"The Fortunate Unhappy".

Daylight and champian discovers not more. This is open. I will be proud, I will read politic authors, I will baffle Sir Toby, I will wash off gross acquaintance, I will be point-devise, the very man. I do not now fool myself, to let imagination jade me, for every reason excites to this, that my lady loves me. She did   130
commend my yellow stockings of late, she did praise my leg being cross-gartered; and in this she manifests herself to my love, and with a kind of injunction drives me to these habits of her liking. I thank my stars, I am happy. I will be strange, stout, in yellow stockings, and cross-gartered, even with the swiftness of putting on. Jove and my stars are praised. Here is yet a postscript.

[Reads] "Thou canst not choose but know who I am. If thou entertain'st my love, let it appear in thy smiling. Thy smiles become thee well. Therefore in my presence still smile, dear my   140
sweet, I prithee."

Jove, I thank thee. I will smile; I will do everything that thou wilt have me.

[Exit]

Section Three
Sub-text in the Lady Macbeth Scenes

This section takes us one stage further, to study a large section of one play—all of the scenes from *Macbeth* in which Lady Macbeth appears. Over the centuries Lady Macbeth has been portrayed in different ways, as: the loving wife, the maternal lady, the sensual lady, the lady possessed, the lady as barbarian, and probably many others. But any interpretation can only be shown in performance—what she does, how she moves, what she says and how she says it.

On the left hand page, instead of the usual scholarly information, are included ideas and questions related to all the elements of the sub-text to encourage discussion and performance.

It is hoped that by this time students will be much more confident and able in tackling a full play in a performance-centred way.

Improvisation

Two people meet to plan a murder. One is fearful, the other determined. Neither is sure what the other is thinking. Improvise the dialogue as they meet.

Text

How will Lady Macbeth enter? Is she reading the letter for the first time? Has she glanced at it and now reads it closely? Has she read it and now experiences what it means? How will your answer affect your reading?

"Hail King that shalt be!" This is the climax of the news. Is it a moment of wonder, excitement, hope, terror, or ferocity? Practise reading the line to reveal these different emotions.

When Lady Macbeth reads "my dearest partner of greatness", is she touched, proud, impatient, or businesslike?

How does she behave during the letter reading? Here is the way one actress played it:

Reinhardt began to read the letter slowly, grew more excited at "missives from the King"; at "Thane of Cawdor" she was checked, read slowly and with surprise until "Hail King. . .". She let the hand that held the letter fall, and for a long silence stared straight ahead. She raised the letter again, read it to the end, let her hand fall again, and in deep abstraction stared ahead.

M. Rosenberg, *Masks of Macbeth*

Look at Lines 13–28 and Lines 40–56. What are possible actions for Lady Macbeth in these speeches?

Line	Action
"Come thick night"	she moves to the window

There is a difficulty in Line 30. Why does she suddenly lose control? She appears to be either frightened or bewildered by the news. How does she react physically to the news?

Scene 1 (Act I, Scene V)
Macbeth has met three witches who prophesy that he will become king of
Scotland. This can only happen with the death of Duncan, the present king.
Macbeth writes to his wife to tell her of the witches.

[Enter Lady Macbeth, reading a letter]

LADY MACBETH: "They met me in the day of success; and I have
    learned by the perfect'st report, they have more in them than
    mortal knowledge. When I burned in desire to question them
    further, they made themselves air, into which they vanished.
    Whiles I stood rapt in the wonder of it, came missives from
    the King, who all-hailed me 'Thane of Cawdor', by which title,
    before these weird sisters saluted me, and referred me to the
    coming on of time with 'Hail King that shalt be!' This have I
    thought good to deliver thee, my dearest partner of greatness,
    that thou mightst not lose the dues of rejoicing by being ignorant   10
    of what greatness is promised thee. Lay it to thy heart, and
    farewell."
    Glamis thou art, and Cawdor, and shalt be
    What thou art promised; yet do I fear thy nature,
    It is too full o' th' milk of human kindness
    To catch the nearest way. Thou wouldst be great,
    Art not without ambition, but without
    The illness should attend it. What thou wouldst highly,
    That wouldst thou holily; wouldst not play false,
    And yet wouldst wrongly win. Thou'dst have, great Glamis,   20
    That which cries "Thus thou must do, if thou have it";
    And that which rather thou dost fear to do
    Than wishest should be undone. Hie thee hither,
    That I may pour my spirits in thine ear,
    And chastise with the valour of my tongue
    All that impedes thee from the golden round,
    Which fate and metaphysical aid doth seem
    To have thee crowned withal.
                    What is your tidings?

MESSENGER: The King comes here tonight.   30
LADY MACBETH: Thou'rt mad to say it.
    Is not thy master with him, who were't so
    Would have informed for preparation.
MESSENGER: So please you, it is true; our Thane is coming.
    One of my fellows had the speed of him
    Who almost dead for breath, had scarcely more
    Than would make up his message.
LADY MACBETH: Give him tending,
    He brings great news.

[Exit attendant]

            The raven himself is hoarse   40

In Lines 40–56, Lady Macbeth calls for help from three sources. Each member of the class chooses one. The teacher asks, "what are you calling for?" and points to a class member. He or she must answer as vividly and as expressively as possible.

Macbeth enters. The main question to consider is: "what is happening between these two people?" They are unsure of each other and about to embark on a terrible crime. Consider the following suggestions for underlining the tension between them:

- Should there be a long silence after Macbeth enters? What would each character do during the silence?
- Can space between the two contribute to the tension?

What is the unspoken meaning of Lines 62–65?

Look at Line 65: "Tomorrow, as he purposes". How many ways are there of saying it. Indifferently? Emphatically? With fear? Quietly? Quickly? Musingly?

In what way would each reading reveal something different going on in Macbeth's mind?

How can Lines 66–76 be read to show Lady Macbeth putting a terrible pressure on Macbeth?

How can the scene end? Which of these do you prefer?
- "We will speak further". Macbeth quickly turns to leave. "Only look up clear": He stops but does not look at his wife. "To alter favour ever is to fear": he listens and leaves. "Leave all the rest to me": Lady Macbeth whispers the line.
- Irving [an actor] preferred a gorgeous exit: she puts her arm around his neck tenderly; he breaks away, as if going off dejected; then turns, puts out his arms, she comes into them, they go off embracing.

M. Rosenberg, *The Masks of Macbeth*

In what ways do the two exits show the different mental states of the characters?

That croaks the fatal entrance of Duncan
Under my battlements. Come you spirits
That tend on mortal thoughts, unsex me here,
And fill me from the crown to the toe top-full
Of direst cruelty; make thick my blood,
Stop up th' access and passage to remorse,
That no compunctious visitings of nature
Shake my fell purpose, nor keep peace between
Th' effect and it. Come to my woman's breasts,
And take my milk for gall, you murd'ring ministers,   50
Wherever in your sightless substances
You wait on nature's mischief. Come thick night,
And pall thee in the dunnest smoke of hell,
That my keen knife see not the wound it makes,
Nor heaven peep through the blanket of the dark,
To cry "Hold, hold!"

[Enter Macbeth]

                      Great Glamis, worthy Cawdor,
Greater than both, by the all-hail hereafter,
Thy letters have transported me beyond
This ignorant present, and I feel now   60
The future in the instant.
MACBETH: My dearest love.
  Duncan comes here tonight.
LADY MACBETH: And when goes hence?
MACBETH: Tomorrow, as he purposes.
LADY MACBETH: O never
Shall sun that morrow see.
Your face, my Thane is as a book where men
May read strange matters. To beguile the time,
Look like the time; bear welcome in your eye,   70
Your hand, your tongue; look like th' innocent flower,
But be the serpent under't. He that's coming
Must be provided for; and you shall put
This night's great business into my despatch,
Which shall to all our nights and days to come
Give solely sovereign sway and masterdom.
MACBETH: We will speak further.
LADY MACBETH: Only look up clear;
To alter favour ever is to fear
Leave all the rest to me.

[Exeunt]

Improvisation

Macbeth is not in this scene. Where is he and what is he thinking? Prepare a monologue of his thoughts at this moment. The following questions may help:

- Does the style sound "thought" or does it sound "spoken aloud" to someone else?
- Does the style seem appropriate to Macbeth and to the situation he is in?
- Does the script "work", when read aloud? Test your reading, preferably with a tape recorder, concentrating on pace, timing, pause, and emphasis.

Write a description of the scene that will convey the atmosphere.

What time of the day is it? What can you make of the torches? Many people enter. In your description try to convey the sense of ceremony and homage. Where is Macbeth at this moment? What is Lady Macbeth doing in the first ten lines? What is she thinking? How is she dressed? How does she approach Duncan? How does she behave towards the King?

Scene 2 (Act I Scene VI)

Duncan arrives at Macbeth's castle to be his guest. He is met by Lady Macbeth.

[Oboes and torches. Enter Duncan, Malcolm, Donalbain, Banquo, Lennox, Macduff, Ross, Angus, and Attendants]

DUNCAN: This castle hath a pleasant seat; the air
    Nimbly and sweetly recommends itself
    Unto our gentle senses.
BANQUO: This guest of summer,
    The temple-haunting martlet, does approve,
    By his loved mansionry, that the heavens' breath
    Smells wooingly here. No jutty, frieze,
    Buttress, nor coign of vantage, but this bird
    Hath made his pendent bed and procreant cradle
    Where they most breed and haunt, I have observed   10
    The air is delicate.

[Enter Lady Macbeth]

DUNCAN: See, see our honoured hostess.
    The love that follows us sometime is our trouble,
    Which still we thank as love. Herein I teach you,
    How you shall bid God 'ild us for your pains,
    And thank us for your trouble.
LADY MACBETH: All our service
    In every point twice done, and then done double,
    Were poor and single business to contend
    Against those honours deep and broad wherewith   20
    Your Majesty loads our house. For those of old,
    And the late dignities heaped up to them,
    We rest your hermits.

Does something in his face check her? Is Duncan going immediately to his death?

Read the scene closely. Do the lines give you some answers to the above questions?

DUNCAN: Where's the Thane of Cawdor?
    We coursed him at the heels, and had a purpose
    To be his purveyor; but he rides well,
    And his great love, sharp as his spur, hath holp him
    To his home before us. Fair and noble hostess,
    We are your guest tonight.
LADY MACBETH: Your servants ever   30
    Have theirs, themselves, and what is theirs, in compt,
    To make their audit at your Highness' pleasure,
    Still to return your own.

    101

Improvisation

Macbeth is trying to abandon the whole project. Choose a Macbeth from the class (the teacher may prefer to act Macbeth). Each student prepares a short statement to attack Macbeth. He replies. Try to deliver the lines taking into account the characters and the situation.

Text

How does Lady Macbeth enter? What does she do?

Look at Lines 11–21. Take Lady Macbeth's first speech and read it in different ways. On each reading alter the tempo, pitch, volume, and emphasis. Settle on the way that feels right for the character and the situation.

Read Lines 22–24. How does Macbeth react to the assault?
The following have been tried by various actors:
- One started to leave and his wife blocked his way.
- One raised an arm in protest.
- One listened with his eyes closed.
- One put his hand over his mouth.
- One buried his knife in the table.

What other possibilities are there?

What is the tone of Lady Macbeth's speech, Lines 25–37? Is it quiet, severe, sarcastic, loving, or threatening?

How many harsh-sounding words are there in the second part of the speech? Will they influence your reading?

What is your opinion of this piece of stage business?

"At 'What beast was't' she had risen to a fierceness that frightened her, and also made her fearful of being overheard. She went quickly to the curtain to see, then hurried back to speak in low tones, sharply.
M. Rosenberg, *The Masks of Macbeth*

What other stage business in her two speeches could help?

Look at line 39, "We fail?". With how many nuances can you say the line: shouting, whispering, hissing, laughing, jeering? Any may be right if really felt and genuinely produced.

DUNCAN: Give me your hand.
Conduct me to mine host, we love him highly,
And shall continue our graces towards him.
By your leave hostess.

[Exeunt]

Scene 3 (Act I, Scene VII)

Duncan has arrived. Lady Macbeth and Macbeth meet. He has been having second thoughts about going through with the murder.

[Macbeth on stage, thinking, Enter Lady Macbeth]

MACBETH: How now? What news?
LADY MACBETH: He has almost supped. Why have you left
the chamber?
MACBETH: Hath he asked for me?
LADY MACBETH: Know you not he has?
MACBETH: We will proceed no further in this business.
He hath honoured me of late, and I have bought
Golden opinions from all sorts of people,
Which would be worn now in their newest gloss,
Not cast aside so soon.   10
LADY MACBETH: Was the hope drunk
Wherein you dressed yourself? Hath it slept since?
And wakes it now to look so green and pale
At what it did so freely? From this time
Such I account thy love. Art thou afeard
To be the same in thine own act and valour
As thou art in desire? Wouldst thou have that
Which thou esteem'st the ornament of life,
And live a coward in thine own esteem,
Letting "I dare not" wait upon "I would,"   20
Like the poor cat i' th' adage?
MACBETH: Prithee peace.
I dare do all that may become a man;
Who dares do more is none.
LADY MACBETH: What beast was't then,
That made you break this enterprise to me?
When you durst do it, then you were a man;
And to be more than what you were, you would
Be so much more the man. Nor time nor place
Did then adhere, and yet you would make both.   30
They have made themselves, and that their fitness now
Does unmake you. I have given suck, and know
How tender 'tis to love the babe that milks me—
I would while it was smiling in my face
Have plucked my nipple from his boneless gums,
And dashed the brains out, had I so sworn as you
Have done to this.

103

The language of Lines 41–50 is softened here with the use of many "M's" "N's" and "W's". How will this influence your reading? What does it show of the character and mental state of Lady Macbeth at this moment?

In what ways can you remind the audience of Duncan? Duncan at this moment is at dinner with his lords. What sound effects and stage business could be useful here? How will the Macbeths react?

How do the Macbeths leave?

Discuss the statement: "The scene is designed to end on a pause of dreadful possibility".

Who is going to kill Duncan?

MACBETH: We will proceed no further with this business.

MACBETH: If we should fail?
LADY MACBETH: We fail?
    But screw your courage to the sticking-place,   40
    And we'll not fail. When Duncan is asleep—
    Whereto the rather shall his day's hard journey
    Soundly invite him—his two chamberlains
    Will I with wine and wassail so convince,
    That memory, the warder of the brain,
    Shall be a fume, and the receipt of reason
    A limbeck only; when in swinish sleep
    Their drenched natures lie as in a death,
    What cannot you and I perform upon
    Th' unguarded Duncan? What not put upon   50
    His spongy officers, who shall bear the guilt
    Of our great quell?
MACBETH: Bring forth men-children only,
    For thy undaunted mettle should compose
    Nothing but males. Will it not be received,
    When we have marked with blood those sleepy two
    Of his own chamber, and used their very daggers,
    That they have done't?
LADY MACBETH: Who dares receive it other,
    As we shall make our griefs and clamour roar   60
    Upon his death?
MACBETH: I am settled, and bend up
    Each corporal agent to this terrible feat.
    Away, and mock the time with fairest show:
    False face must hide what the false heart doth know.

                        [Exeunt]

Improvisation

Who is going to kill Duncan? Look at the following possibilities:

- Have Macbeth go in to kill the king. He comes out and meets his wife. Develop the dialogue.
- Have Lady Macbeth go in to kill the king. She comes out and meets her husband. Develop the dialogue.
- We do not see the murder of the king. Mime the murder.

Text

Long silences in the first fourteen lines could create suspense. Where would you put them?

"Had he not resembled . . ." (Line 13). Is this an important line in judging the character of Lady Macbeth? What other lines in the first speeches also show her character? What movements and gestures here can also show her character?

Read closely Lines 1–14. Note how Lady Macbeth's thoughts constantly change. How should this influence a reading?

How does Macbeth enter after Line 14? There are many possibilities: one actor staggered backwards from the murder room; another blindly stumbled down the steps: another's gestures and movements were out of control.

What other possibilities are there?

What can you make of the short lines in Lines 15–26?

Scene 4 (Act II, Scene II)
Macbeth has entered Duncan's chamber to murder him. Lady Macbeth waits
for her husband.

[Enter Lady Macbeth]

LADY MACBETH: That which hath made them drunk hath
   made me bold;
   What hath quenched them hath given me fire. Hark! Peace!
   It was the owl that shrieked, the fatal bellman,
   Which gives the stern'st good night. He is about it.
   The doors are open; and the surfeited grooms
   Do mock their charge with snores. I have drugged their possets.
   That death and nature do contend about them,
   Whether they live or die.
MACBETH: *[Within]*   Who's there? What ho!
LADY MACBETH: Alack, I am afraid they have awaked,   10
   And 'tis not done. Th' attempt and not the deed
   Confounds us. Hark! I laid their daggers ready,
   He could not miss 'em. Had he not resembled
   My father as he slept, I had done't.

[Enter Macbeth]

            My husband!
MACBETH: I have done the deed. Didst thou not hear a noise?
LADY MACBETH: I heard the owl scream and the crickets cry.
   Did not you speak?
MACBETH: When?
LADY MACBETH: Now.   20
MACBETH: As I descended?
LADY MACBETH: Ay.
MACBETH: Hark!
   Who lies i' th' second chamber?
LADY MACBETH: Donalbain.
MACBETH: This is a sorry sight.

[Looks on his hands]

LADY MACBETH: A foolish thought, to say a sorry sight.
MACBETH: There's one did laugh in's sleep, and one cried
   "Murder!"
   That they did wake each other. I stood and heard them.   30
   But they did say their prayers, and addressed them
   Again to sleep.
LADY MACBETH: There are two lodged together.
MACBETH: One cried "God bless us!" and "Amen!" the other,
   As they had seen me with these hangman's hands.
   Listening their fear, I could not say "Amen,"
   When they did say "God bless us!"
LADY MACBETH: Consider it not so deeply.

Look at Lines 44–53. One critic claims that from "Methought I heard. . ." to "Macbeth shall sleep. . ." there is a rise in intensity reaching a climax of distress. Would you agree? Are there other ways of reading it?

Why did Macbeth bring the daggers from the murder? (Line 58). What does he do on the suggestion that he return to the murder scene? Here is how some actors have played it:

Kean refused to return with shuddering agony.
Rossi could only look at his wife in horror.
Matkowsky started back with a cry. McKellen retched.

M. Rosenberg, The Masks of Macbeth

Read Lines 65–70. How does Lady Macbeth return to the murder? What does Macbeth do while she is gone?

How do they leave?

What happens next?

MACBETH: But wherefore could not I pronounce "Amen"?
I had most need of blessing, and "Amen"   40
Stuck in my throat.

LADY MACBETH: These deeds must not be thought
After these ways; so, it will make us mad.

MACBETH: Methought I heard a voice cry "Sleep no more!"
Macbeth does murder sleep, the innocent sleep,
Sleep that knits up the ravelled sleave of care,
The death of each day's life, sore labour's bath,
Balm of hurt minds, great nature's second course,
Chief nourisher in life's feast.

LADY MACBETH: What do you mean?   50

MACBETH: Still it cried "Sleep no more!" to all the house.
Glamis hath murdered sleep, and therefore Cawdor
Shall sleep no more, Macbeth shall sleep no more.

LADY MACBETH: Who was it that thus cried? Why worthy Thane,
You do unbend your noble strength, to think
So brainsickly of things. Go get some water,
And wash this filthy witness from your hand.
Why did you bring these daggers from the place?
They must lie there. Go carry them, and smear
The sleepy grooms with blood.   60

MACBETH: I'll go no more.
I am afraid to think what I have done.
Look on't again I dare not.

LADY MACBETH: Infirm of purpose!
Give me the daggers. The sleeping and the dead
Are but as pictures. 'Tis the eye of childhood
That fears a painted devil. If he do bleed,
I'll gild the faces of the grooms withal,
For it must seem their guilt.

[Exit. Knock within]

MACBETH: Whence is that knocking?   70
How is't with me, when every noise appals me?
What hands are here? Ha! They pluck out mine eyes.
Will all great Neptune's ocean wash this blood
Clean from my hand? No, this my hand will rather
The multitudinous seas incarnadine,
Making the green one red.

[Enter Lady Macbeth]

LADY MACBETH: My hands are of your colour; but I shame
To wear a heart so white. *[Knock within]* I hear a knocking
At the south entry. Retire we to our chamber.
A little water clears us of this deed.   80
How easy is it then! Your constancy
Hath left you unattended. *[Knock within]* Hark, more knocking.

Improvisation

Write the lines of the scene in your own words.

Text	Modern Version
Lines 13–14. "Things without all remedy…"	We should take no notice of things we cannot do anything about
Lines 24–25. "Duncan is in his grave…"	Duncan is dead. He is happy now that he has escaped life's problems.

The best way to compare the two versions is to read them aloud, preferably into a tape recorder.

Text

The text suggests they see and talk to each other at once. But is this necessary? What stage business can show the deep despair of both people? For example can silence suggest that anguish? What would they do during the silence?

How does Macbeth behave in this scene? Would you agree with the following comment by a critic? "This scene gives Macbeth the best chance, in words and action, to show a husband's quiet affection".

What is Lady Macbeth's attitude to Macbeth in this scene—gentle, caring, harsh, scolding? How will your answer influence the reading of her lines?

Read Lines 24–28. Some commentators think that the many "F's" and "S's" suggest the lines should be whispered. Do you agree?

Two actors played the line "O full of scorpions…" (Line 40) very differently. One showed a physical anguish—savagely biting his lip, his fist beating at his forehead. Another quietly turned to his wife for consolation. Which do you prefer? What other possibilities are there?

How do they leave at the end of the scene? Embracing? Staring at each other in horror? Together? Separately? Experiment with these exits and others that may be suggested.

Get on your nightgown, lest occasion call us,
And show us to be watchers. Be not lost
So poorly in your thoughts.
MACBETH: To know my deed, 'twere best not know myself.

[Knock within]

Wake Duncan with thy knocking. I would thou couldst.

[Exeunt]

Scene 5 (Act III, Scene II)
Macbeth is in anguish over the murder but he is determined to go on. His wife tries to comfort him.

[Enter Lady Macbeth and a Servant]

LADY MACBETH: Is Banquo gone from Court?
SERVANT: Ay madam, but returns again tonight.
LADY MACBETH: Say to the King, I would attend his leisure
   For a few words.
SERVANT: /   Madam I will.

[Exit]

LADY MACBETH: Nought's had, all's spent,
   Where our desire is got without content.
   'Tis safer to be that which we destroy,
   Than by destruction dwell in doubtful joy.

[Enter Macbeth]

How now my lord? Why do you keep alone,   10
Of sorriest fancies your companions making,
Using those thoughts which should indeed have died
With them they think on? Things without all remedy
Should be without regard: what's done is done.
MACBETH: We have scorched the snake, not killed it:
   She'll close, and be herself, whilst our poor malice
   Remains in danger of her former tooth.
   But let the frame of things disjoint, both the worlds suffer,
   Ere we will eat our meal in fear, and sleep
   In the affliction of these terrible dreams   20
   That shake us nightly. Better be with the dead,
   Whom we, to gain our peace, have sent to peace,
   Than on the torture of the mind to lie
   In restless ecstasy. Duncan is in his grave,
   After life's fitful fever he sleeps well,
   Treason has done his worst: nor steel, nor poison,
   Malice domestic, foreign levy, nothing,
   Can touch him further.
LADY MACBETH: Come on.
   Gentle my lord, sleek o'er your rugged looks,   30
   Be bright and jovial among your guests tonight.

Improvisation

Act out the proceedings of the banquet up to the appearance of the ghost. There will be nobles standing around talking, servants preparing the table and pouring wine, while Macbeth moves around the room. The more jollity there is the more stark will be the later events.

Text

There will be much happening during Lines 20–38.

Reinhardt's Macbeth was about to drink, the bowl in his hand. For some seconds he stood still, as if turned to stone, then backed off. He saw Banquo. The ghost's throat was cut and its forehead, also gashed, had intimations of the Crucifixion. As Macbeth spoke, in a suffocated voice, the ghost raised a threatening hand.

M. Rosenberg, *Masks of Macbeth*

But what are the others doing?:
- Lady Macbeth?
- The other guests?
- The guards?

MACBETH: So shall I, love, and so I pray be you.
    Let your remembrance apply to Banquo,
    Present him eminence both with eye and tongue—
    Unsafe the while that we
    Must lave our honours in these flattering streams,
    And make our faces vizards to our hearts,
   ·Disguising what they are.
LADY MACBETH: You must leave this.
MACBETH: O full of scorpions is my mind, dear wife.   40
    Thou know'st that Banquo, and his Fleance, lives.
LADY MACBETH: But in them nature's copy's not eterne.
MACBETH: There's comfort yet, they are assailable;
    Then be thou jocund. Ere the bat hath flown
    His cloistered flight, ere to black Hecate's summons
    The shard-borne beetle with his drowsy hums
    Hath rung night's yawning peal, there shall be done
    A deed of dreadful note.
LADY MACBETH: What's to be done?
MACBETH: Be innocent of the knowledge, dearest chuck,   50
    Till thou applaud the deed. Come seeling night,
    Scarf up the tender eye of pitiful day,
    And with thy bloody and invisible hand
    Cancel and tear to pieces the great bond
    Which keeps me pale. Light thickens, and the crow
    Makes wing to th' rooky wood.
    Good things of day begin to droop and drowse,
    Whiles night's black agents to their preys do rouse.
    Thou marvell'st at my words; but hold thee still,
    Things bad begun make strong themselves by ill.   60
    So prithee go with me.

[Exeunt]

Scene 6 (Act III, Scene IV)
Macbeth has just had Banquo, a noble, murdered because he fears he is
a threat to his position. He has been crowned and hosts a banquet for the
nobles of Scotland. Banquo's ghost appears.

[A banquet prepared. Enter Macbeth, Lady Macbeth, Ross,
Lennox, Lords, and Attendants]

MACBETH: You know your own degrees, sit down. At first
    And last the hearty welcome.
LORDS: Thanks to your Majesty.
MACBETH: Ourself will mingle with society,
    And play the humble host.
    Our hostess keeps her state, but in best time
    We will require her welcome.
LADY MACBETH: Pronounce it for me sir, to all our friends,
    For my heart speaks they are welcome.

Read Lines 40–50. Is Lady Macbeth frightened, scornful, or angry? How can she be sure the guests do not hear her?

How in gesture, movement, and voice can Lady Macbeth be portrayed both as fearful wife and helpful hostess, throughout the passage Lines 30–50? One actress rebuked Macbeth angrily, then looking at his terrified face clapped her hands together. The sound makes the guests look at them. What happens then?

As Macbeth speaks Lines 50–60, is he desperate, hysterical, or brave? One actor whispered the speech while backing away. But another, on the line "Why what care I?" broke through the guests and grabbed anything to hand—food, plates, goblets—and hurled them at the ghost. What other possibilities are there?

[Enter first Murderer to the door]

MACBETH: See, they encounter thee with their hearts' thanks. 10
    Both sides are even, here I'll sit i' th' midst.
    Be large in mirth, anon we'll drink a measure
    The table round.
    Now, good digestion wait on appetite,
    And health on both.
LENNOX: May't please your Highness sit.

[The Ghost of Banquo enters, and sits in Macbeth's seat]

MACBETH: Here had we now our country's honour roofed,
    Were the graced person of our Banquo present;
    Who may I rather challenge for unkindness,
    Than pity for mischance. 20
ROSS: His absence sir,
    Lays blame upon his promise. Please't your Highness
    To grace us with your royal company.
MACBETH: The table's full.
LENNOX: Here is a place reserved, sir.
MACBETH: Where?
LENNOX: Here my good lord. What is't that moves your
    Highness?
MACBETH: Which of you have done this?
LORDS: What, my good lord?
MACBETH: Thou canst not say I did it; never shake 30
    Thy gory locks at me.
ROSS: Gentlemen rise, his Highness is not well.
LADY MACBETH: Sit worthy friends. My lord is often thus,
    And hath been from his youth. Pray you keep seat,
    The fit is momentary, upon a thought
    He will again be well. If much you note him,
    You shall offend him, and extend his passion.
    Feed, and regard him not—Are you a man?
MACBETH: Ay, and a bold one, that dare look on that
    Which might appal the devil. 40
LADY MACBETH: O proper stuff!
    This is the very painting of your fear.
    This is the air-drawn dagger which you said
    Led you to Duncan. O these flaws and starts,
    Impostors to true fear, would well become
    A woman's story at a winter's fire,
    Authorized by her grandam. Shame itself,
    Why do you make such faces? When all's done,
    You look but on a stool.
MACBETH: Prithee see there. Behold, look, lo, how say you? 50
    Why what care I? If thou canst nod, speak too.
    If charnel-houses and our graves must send
    Those that we bury back, our monuments

There seem to be at least three possible interpretations for Lines 78–90:
- A frightened Macbeth retreats
- A determined Macbeth stands his ground
- A maddened Macbeth attacks

How will your decision affect how the speech is said, or what Macbeth does? This is how one actor played it:

As Sothern gathered courage, he thrust forward with his sword, as if through the ghost. Sothern dropped his sword, fell on his knees, and beat at the stool with clenched hands, hysterically, until it fell over. The company shrank from him in fright.

M. Rosenberg, *The Masks of Macbeth*

Shall be the maws of kites.

[Ghost disappears]

LADY MACBETH: What, quite unmanned in folly?

MACBETH: If I stand here, I saw him.

LADY MACBETH: Fie for shame!

MACBETH: Blood hath been shed ere now, i' th' olden time,
Ere humane statute purged the gentle weal;
Ay, and since too, murders have been performed   60
Too terrible for the ear. The time has been,
That when the brains were out, the man would die,
And there an end. But now they rise again.
With twenty mortal murders on their crowns,
And push us from our stools. This is more strange
Than such a murder is.

LADY MACBETH: My worthy lord,
Your noble friends do lack you.

MACBETH: I do forget.
Do not muse at me, my most worthy friends,   70
I have a strange infirmity, which is nothing
To those that know me. Come, love and health to all,
Then I'll sit down. Give me some wine, fill full.
I drink to the general joy o' the whole table,

[Enter Ghost]

And to our dear friend Banquo, whom we miss;
Would he were here. To all, and him, we thirst,
And all to all.

LORDS: Our duties, and the pledge.

MACBETH: Avaunt, and quit my sight, let the earth hide thee!
Thy bones are marrowless, thy blood is cold;   80
Thou hast no speculation in those eyes
Which thou dost glare with!

LADY MACBETH: Think of this good peers,
But as a thing of custom. 'Tis no other,
Only it spoils the pleasure of the time.

MACBETH: What man dare, I dare.
Approach thou like the rugged Russian bear,
The armed rhinoceros, or the Hyrcan tiger;
Take any shape but that, and my firm nerves
Shall never tremble. Or be alive again,   90
And dare me to the desert with thy sword;
If trembling I inhabit then, protest me
The baby of a girl. Hence horrible shadow,
Unreal mockery, hence!

[Ghost disappears]

Why, so; being gone,
I am a man again. Pray you sit still.

What is achieved by breaking Line 110 after "But go..." with a long pause and then shouting out the order "at once"?

Look at Lines 113–119. The guests have left. Lady Macbeth must be mentally exhausted. How can you show their weariness and disillusionment? Will long silences help? One production had them crouching together; suddenly they burst out sobbing. Another had Lady Macbeth apart from Macbeth, watching him as he sat staring. Which do you prefer? What other possibilities are there?

Do you agree that the last speeches in this scene (Lines 113–137) need several changes in tone?

How do Macbeth and Lady Macbeth leave?

What is going to happen to Lady Macbeth now? Improvise the next scene you think she will appear in.

LADY MACBETH: You have displaced the mirth, broke the
    good meeting
    With most admired disorder.
MACBETH: Can such things be,
    And overcome us like a summer's cloud,   100
    Without our special wonder? You make me strange
    Even to the disposition that I owe,
    When now I think you can behold such sights,
    And keep the natural ruby of your cheeks,
    When mine is blanched with fear.
ROSS: What sights, my lord?
LADY MACBETH: I pray you speak not; he grows worse and worse.
    Question enrages him. At once, good night.
    Stand not upon the order of your going.
    But go at once.   110
LENNOX: Good night, and better health
    Attend his Majesty.
LADY MACBETH: A kind good night to all.

[Exeunt all but Macbeth and Lady Macbeth]

MACBETH: It will have blood, they say; blood will have blood.
    Stones have been known to move, and trees to speak.
    Augures and understood relations have
    By magot-pies and choughs and rooks brought forth
    The secret'st man of blood. What is the night?
LADY MACBETH: Almost at odds with morning, which is which.
MACBETH: How say'st thou, that Macduff denies his person   120
    At our great bidding?
LADY MACBETH: Did you send to him sir?
MACBETH: I hear it by the way; but I will send.
    There's not a one of them but in his house
    I keep a servant fee'd. I will tomorrow,
    And betimes I will, to the Weird Sisters.
    More shall they speak; for now I am bent to know
    By the worst means, the worst, for mine own good.
    All causes shall give way. I am in blood
    Stepped in so far, that should I wade no more,   130
    Returning were as tedious as go o'er.
    Strange things I have in head, that will to hand;
    Which must be acted ere they may be scanned.
LADY MACBETH: You lack the season of all natures, sleep.
MACBETH: Come, we'll to sleep. My strange and self-abuse
    Is the initiate fear, that wants hard use.
    We are yet but young in deed.

[Exeunt]

Improvisation

Lady Macbeth suicides soon after this scene. Write her death soliloquy and improvise the suicide scene.

Text

Where will the observers hide? How will they speak?

How will Lady Macbeth look physically?

How does Lady Macbeth enter? Is her walk slow, quick, hesitant, like that of a blind person?

Lady Macbeth does a great deal in this scene. Though she has no visual sense, she seems to "see" a great deal, as well as hear, smell, touch and perhaps even taste. What lines suggest these sensations?

How does she rub her hands?

How does she speak—in whispers, wailing, moaning, or screaming? Or perhaps all of these?

"Out damned spot" (Line 32): one actress whispered it; another spoke with a shuddering sigh, another fell back shrieking hysterically. Practise these and other readings and decide which is the most convincing.

Some critics claim that Lines 38–40 are the saddest lines in the scene. Do you agree?

What does Lady Macbeth do while the doctor is talking?

Scene 7 (Act V, Scene I)
Some time has passed. Macbeth continues to murder any who oppose him.
In her conscience-stricken grief Lady Macbeth constantly sleepwalks. A
doctor is called in to watch her one evening.

[Enter a Doctor of Physic and a Waiting Gentlewoman]

DOCTOR: I have two nights watched with you, but can perceive
no truth in your report. When was it she last walked?

GENTLEWOMAN: Since his Majesty went into the field, I have
seen her rise from her bed, throw her nightgown upon her,
unlock her closet, take forth paper, fold it, write upon't, read
it, afterwards seal it, and again return to bed; yet all this while in a
most fast sleep.

DOCTOR: A great perturbation in nature, to receive at once
the benefit of sleep, and do the effects of watching. In this
slumbery agitation, besides her walking, and other actual   10
performances, what at any time have you heard her say?

GENTLEWOMAN: That sir, which I will not report after her.

DOCTOR: You may to me, and 'tis most meet you should.

GENTLEWOMAN: Neither to you nor any one, having no
witness to confirm my speech.

[Enter Lady Macbeth with a taper]

Lo you, here she comes. This is her very guise, and upon my
life fast asleep.
Observe her, stand close.

DOCTOR: How came she by that light?   20

GENTLEWOMAN: Why it stood by her. She has light by her
continually, 'tis her command.

DOCTOR: You see her eyes are open.

GENTLEWOMAN: Ay but their sense is shut.

DOCTOR: What is it she does now? Look how she rubs her
hands.

GENTLEWOMAN: It is an accustomed action with her, to seem
thus washing her hands. I have known her continue in this a
quarter of an hour.

LADY MACBETH: Yet here's a spot.

DOCTOR: Hark! she speaks. I will set down what comes from   30
her, to satisfy my remembrance the more strongly.

LADY MACBETH: Out damned spot, out I say! One, two; why
then 'tis time to do't. Hell is murky. Fie my lord, fie! A
soldier, and afeard? What need we fear who knows it, when
none can call our power to account? Yet who would have
thought the old man to have had so much blood in him?

DOCTOR: Do you mark that?

LADY MACBETH: The Thane of Fife had a wife; where is she
now? What, will these hands ne'er be clean? No more o' that
my lord, no more o' that: you mar all with this starting.   40

121

How can you best achieve the horror and pathos of the end? This is what happened in three performances:

Vanbrugh could only whisper the last words tonelessly, as weary to death, she dragged herself back along the high, narrow stairs. Campbell left with a low, long, mournful cry, desolate, despairing, tortured. The desperate Annis, when her outstretched hand found the old Doctor, took him for Macbeth and tried to drag him with her.

M. Rosenberg, *The Masks of Macbeth*

DOCTOR: Go to, go to! You have known what you should not.

GENTLEWOMAN: She has spoke what she should not, I am
sure of that. Heaven knows what she has known.

LADY MACBETH: Here's the smell of the blood still; all the
perfumes of Arabia will not sweeten this little hand. Oh, oh,
oh!

DOCTOR: What a sigh is there! The heart is sorely charged.

GENTLEWOMAN: I would not have such a heart in my bosom
for the dignity of the whole body.

DOCTOR: Well, well, well.   50

GENTLEWOMAN: Pray God it be sir.

DOCTOR: This disease is beyond my practice. Yet I have known
those which have walked in their sleep who have died holily
in their beds.

LADY MACBETH: Wash your hands, put on your nightgown,
look not so pale. I tell you yet again Banquo's buried; he can
not come out on's grave.

DOCTOR: Even so?

LADY MACBETH: To bed, to bed; there's knocking at the gate.
Come, come, come, come, give me your hand. What's done   60
cannot be undone. To bed, to bed, to bed.

[Exit]

DOCTOR: Will she go now to bed?

GENTLEWOMAN: Directly.

DOCTOR: Foul whisperings are abroad. Unnatural deeds
Do breed unnatural troubles; infected minds
To their deaf pillows will discharge their secrets.
More needs she the divine than the physician.
God, God forgive us all. Look after her,
Remove from her the means of all annoyance,
And still keep eyes upon her. So, good night: 70
My mind she has mated, and amazed my sight.
I think, but dare not speak.

GENTLEWOMAN: Good night good doctor.

[Exeunt]